Louisiana Bicentennial Reprint Series

Louisiana Bicentennial Reprint Series

JOSEPH G. TREGLE, JR., General Editor

The History of Louisiana,
translated from the French of M. Le Page du Pratz
JOSEPH G. TREGLE, JR., Editor

The Manhattaner in New Orleans:
Or, Phases of "Crescent City" Life,
by A. Oakey Hall
HENRY A. KMEN, Editor

Norman's New Orleans and Environs,
by Benjamin Moore Norman
MATTHEW J. SCHOTT, Editor

THE MANHATTANER IN NEW ORLEANS

The

MANHATTANER

in

NEW ORLEANS

OR, PHASES OF "CRESCENT CITY" LIFE

A. Oakey Hall

Edited by Henry A. Kmen

Published for the
Louisiana American Revolution
Bicentennial Commission
by the
Louisiana State University Press
Baton Rouge

LIBRARY OF CONGRESS CATALOGING IN PUBLICATION DATA

Hall, Abraham Oakey, 1826–1898.
  The Manhattaner in New Orleans.

  (Louisiana bicentennial reprint series)
  "A facsimile reproduction of the 1851 edition, with foreword, introduction, and index added."
  1. New Orleans—Social life and customs—Addresses, essays, lectures. 2. New Orleans—Description—Addresses, essays, lectures. I. Louisiana American Revolution Bicentennial Commission. II. Title. III. Series.
F379.N55H34 1976   976.3'35   75–21960
ISBN 0–8071–0167–2

CONTENTS

FOREWORD

N O CITY in the world caught the imagination and fixed the interest of early nineteenth-century America as did New Orleans. Its fascination was a mixture of many elements: Latin, foreign in its origins, mysterious in its responses and in its customs, the Crescent City was the concentration of that exotic, non–Anglo-Saxon civilization which Jefferson's Louisiana Purchase had attached to an uncertain Republic. Sensuous, chromatic, redolent, sybaritic, the city's very "wickedness" exerted an almost irresistible pull on more staid and puritanical neo-brethren to the north. Physicians from outside yearned to do battle with the fearful mortality of the "Wet Grave." Divines everywhere were tempted to strap on the harness of righteousness to crush sin in the Babylon of the Lower Mississippi Valley. And withal, at a time when America was more and more preoccupied with accumulation of national and personal fortune, New Orleans stood astride the great artery of commerce of the whole western interior. As much as the citizens of the metropolis themselves, Americans generally, in the 1840s, were convinced that in a relatively short time the already booming port was to become a mercantile mart of a munificence and grandeur beyond anything the world had ever known. Cupidity cast the strongest lure of all.

It was to accommodate this pervasive attraction that A. Oakey Hall wrote the articles known as *The Manhattaner in New Orleans*. Combining the curiosity of the outsider with the insights of an almost-native, Hall was ideally equipped for the task, and his constantly entertaining and informative sketches retain their charm and freshness even today. The ebullience of his pages also reminds us how firmly the nascent Republic had seized on its still-young independence as early as the 1840s. The American Revolution had been sealed by the great victory at Chalmette in 1815: Hall's generation was secure in its vision of the future, and nowhere did that vision glow so brightly as in the Queen City of New Orleans.

Henry A. Kmen, Professor of History at Tulane University, has long been a student of the social and cultural heritage of the city. His *Music in New Orleans* is the standard work in its field, and preparing that study gave Professor Kmen a particularly broad overview from which to introduce *The Manhattaner* with understanding and perception. To the reader's advantage, Kmen joins Hall in the recognition that New Orleans is to be savored and enjoyed as well as studied.

JOSEPH G. TREGLE, JR.

INTRODUCTION

ABRAHAM OAKEY HALL was born in Albany, New York, on July 26, 1826. He was one of twins, but his sister died soon after birth. Although the babies were born in New York State their mother was a resident of New Orleans. She had undertaken a special trip north so that her children might be born under her father's roof. As soon after the births as was possible she rejoined her husband, Morgan James Hall, in New Orleans, where he had a business bearing the name of Hall and Kemp. Mrs. Hall's brother, Samuel Oakey, had emigrated to New Orleans about 1819 and had prospered in cotton. So the newborn A. Oakey Hall had strong early ties to New Orleans and might have grown up there had it not been that in the summer of 1830, his father died of yellow fever in Charleston, South Carolina, while on a business trip.

To escape further contact with the dread disease, Oakey Hall's mother took the four-year-old Oakey and a recently born sister north to New York, where her husband's parents lived. Not very well off, she nevertheless managed to send her son to good schools. He proved to be quite bright, and in the fall of 1840, when he was only fourteen, he matriculated at New York University. While there he wrote for the *Evening Signal and Tatler*, the *Aurora*, and the *Evening Mirror*. His writing included essays on government, book reviews, dramatic criticisms, police reports, and the like. In short, he was developing into an all-around newspaper man.

Hall was graduated in July, 1844, and entered Harvard Law School in the fall, with the financial help of his uncle in New Orleans, Samuel Oakey. But for some reason he left Harvard at the end of one term, perhaps because he found it too slow, or simply because he wanted to be elsewhere. At any rate, for the next few months he read law at the offices of Charles W. Sanford in New York. Then he went to New Orleans to live with his uncle and to continue his preparation for the bar under John Slidell.

In 1846 Oakey Hall was examined by a group of lawyers that included Judah P. Benjamin and was admitted to legal practice. (Benjamin and Hall became good friends and remained so until Benjamin's death in 1884.) But a fledgling lawyer usually needs some money to get started, and Hall drew on his previous newspaper experience. He began to write for the New Orleans *Delta* and the New Orleans *Commercial Bulletin*. In addition he wrote extended pieces for a new and ambitious literary magazine in New York, the *Literary World*. These

pieces were usually titled "The Manhattaner in New
Orleans," and in 1851 most of the articles, plus two later
additions, were gathered together and published by J. S.
Redfield in New York and J. C. Morgan in New Orleans.
The book was dedicated to Hall's uncle, Samuel W.
Oakey, and bore the title of *The Manhattaner in New
Orleans: Or, Phases of "Crescent City" Life*.

It is a book that can be read purely for pleasure by
anyone interested in antebellum New Orleans or, for
that matter, in antebellum America. But its principal
function is as a source for American history; and, although the author's own future was to be filled with
politics, what Hall gives us here is social history. Bar-
bara Tuchman has written of the "corroborative detail
that giveth life to history." Hall's book is simply full of
such detail. He is especially good at evoking atmosphere,
at giving us a sense of being there.

The book begins with Hall's first sight of the mouth of
the Mississippi River and the surrounding landscape. He
then pokes fun at the steam tugboat that was supposed to
pull his packet upriver the next day. The voyage took
twenty hours, during which time Hall observed well the
plantations and other farms that lined the river on both
sides. He was especially taken by the groves of orange
and cyprus trees. But the harbor and levees engaged
Hall's attention in particular, and he was astonished to
see so much of the port's business and goods atop the
levee.

Hall was even more struck by the renowned St.
Charles Hotel, though he was depressed to see the

numerous hog pens clustered around the hostelry. It reminded him, he wrote, of a "mammoth pearl thrown before swine," and Hall appealed to the city fathers to clean out the area around the St. Charles. His concern here was as a resident as well as a reporter. But it is the reporter who makes us feel the emptiness that hung over the great hotel during late August and September when the threat of yellow fever drove so many away. Hall himself went "through the Yellow Fever ordeal" and so could write about it at firsthand. In sharp contrast was the activity in January, as the hotel fed two or three hundred "individual bachelors and exiled married ones." On other nights there were large gatherings of more or less upper-class families who, among other things, sought to find a suitable match for their daughters.

Every now and then Hall departs from straight description to wax eloquent and to philosophize over such things as the dreams and fate of the residents of the St. Charles. These passages may tell us little of New Orleans, but they tell us much about the literary demands of the age. Such philosophical flights and fancies were required in the journalism of those days. But Hall has his feet on the ground again when he describes those other leading hotels, the Verandah and the St. Louis. He is rather harsh on the aristocratic pride of the French Creoles, saying that he would never "hear of the St. Louis hotel without thinking of dirty shirts and moustaches."

Food was already an item of note in New Orleans and Hall advises the visitor that he can find a cafe or restaurateur on every block, as well as oyster stands and barroom counters. They all served liquor, and Hall's description of the bars and saloons that lined the streets from the St. Charles Hotel up two blocks toward Lafayette Square, in an atmosphere "redolent of oysters and lunches, juleps and punches," makes one wish to have walked that two blocks at least once in his life.

In the midst of this inviting area stood a fairly new Exchange, intended by its builders for literary and commercial discussions. But within a year it had become a drinking place as well and sported a bar at least fifty feet long. Oakey Hall approved the change, arguing that in New Orleans drinking and literature "touch noses in cosy friendship." As proof of this he offers us a trip to Morgan's bar and literary haven in full swing. Here were all the newspapers one could want, plus novels and magazines, among them Hall's own articles in *Literary World*.

It was both gratifying and profitable to be published, and so Hall continued to submit his observations and opinions of New Orleans as the city was in the late 1840s. There is a good chapter on the city government, which at the time was divided into three autonomous municipal districts. There is Hall's assessment of the Creoles, whom he found to be "narrow, dark and dirty." And there is much on the weather and mud—in fact there is an entire chapter on the climate. Here one should remember that although the weather in New Orleans was the same then as it is now, ways of coping with it were very different, and one still profits much from reading of how the weather and climate affected the people in those days.

Equally valuable are accounts, for example, like the one explaining the science of getting beneath the mosquito netting of the bed without letting in swarms of hungry pursuers. This task required brains as well as speed and agility, for one often had to begin attacking on one side of the bed to lure most of the pests to that quarter, at which time a quick move to the other side gave unaccompanied admission beneath the netting. It remained now to deal with those mosquitoes who, undeceived, had gotten inside the barrier. These had to be carefully assassinated, one by one. In a similar vein Hall conveys the feeling about and reaction to yellow fever in New Orleans prior to the great epidemics of 1853 and 1857. He describes what it was like to contract the dread disease and live through his own bout with it.

As a lawyer, Hall was keenly aware of being in the only state that practiced civil law, a state where "the sublime teachings of the Pandects school the operations of the most commercial community in the New World." He gives us a vivid picture of the normal activities in and around the old Court House and describes knowingly the pitfalls that civil law held for Americans from other states who thought they could continue the legal ways they had inherited and brought with them from the North. It is perhaps for them that Hall outlines the practical procedures of going to trial.

In Hall's opinion, public morality in New Orleans was purer "than in any other American city." Thefts, fights, street rowdies, he thought, were encountered much less frequently than in Boston or Philadelphia. He finds religion to be at a discount, however, and one of his passages gives a superb sketch of a Sunday in New Orleans in the 1840s: the theaters and opera open; bull-baiting and balloon aeronauts vying for audiences; cavalry, firemen, and infantry all jostling each other; and crowds of merchants thronging the post office lobbies at noon.

It is doubly interesting, in view of recent complaints about loafers and panhandlers in Jackson Square (then called the Place d'Armes), to see the park characterized by Hall as a Sunday haven for "arriving immigrants, drunken sailors, and lazy stevedores." Hall pleads that by "a judicious expenditure" of a few thousand dollars the square might be made an inviting promenade. It would seem that his advice finally is being followed.

What Hall seems to do best is take you there with him, making you see the sights and hear the sounds, even smell the smells and feel the weather. All of these sensations were combined at the opera, and Hall swore that nowhere else in the country could he be satisfied with the genre after having worn out several coats at the Orleans Theater.

This was not just one man's opinion—Hall was right, and his remarks about the opera in New Orleans are as good a critical summing-up as one will find. And this is important, because the French Opera in New Orleans was by any measure the finest in North America. It was the first resident, truly top-class company; and visitors from all over Europe came to see, hear, and praise it. Its six tours of the Northeast in 1827–1833 did much to broaden musical horizons in that region. Cities like Philadelphia were introduced to instruments never heard before, like the bassoon. But most of all they heard the best European operas performed in a manner better than that known in Europe outside of Paris or Vienna. This magnificent achievement was in its greatest period when Hall was a steady patron, making his remarks all the more cogent.

Hall correctly realized that the ensemble was the strength of the company; there was not just an occasional fine soloist surrounded by hacks and squeaky orchestras, as was all too often the case elsewhere. Here were "none of your spasmodic or mongrel affairs," none of your half-and-half orchestras and singers, and none of your choruses made up of a motley crew of "under bandits, sextons, smugglers, dragoons, and comedy waiters." Instead, here one found "always good management; always good singing; always good instrumentation in the orchestra; always an agreeable, fashionable, and critical audience."

Outside the opera house and once again at the Place d'Armes, we see the "temporary print galleries" around the iron railings, much as they are today. Hall was fond of strolling around the city and describing what he encountered. On one of these journeys he notes what he calls the St. Giles of New Orleans, a district where "poverty and vice run races with want and passion," the depravity of which would challenge that of New York or any other city. Further on he passed the Branch Mint Building on

Esplanade and eventually swung over to Congo Square
(then called Circus Square) where he saw crowds of
slaves and onlookers shaking the soil with "dancing or
jumping." The instruments Hall depicts here are all
primitive, handmade from bones and barrels, and probably derived from West Indies instruments. But there
were also banjos and violins in the festivities. In another
week, when the square was the site of a circus, Hall saw a
band that consisted of four trombones and a drum.

A favorite watering place of the people in New Orleans
was on the shore of Lake Pontchartrain at the end of a
little railroad. The train started at Decatur Street and
ran out Elysian Fields to the lake. Hall makes fun of all
this, jeering that the engine had one thousand
mosquito-power, was a relic from the infantile days of
steam propulsion, and ran over a "primitive remnant of
railway navigation" for about four miles through sand
and grass and swamp thicket. But once over the disagreeable little trip, one could board a steamer at the
lake front bound for other watering places like Bay St.
Louis, Pass Christian, Pascagoula, and Pensacola. Hall's
favorite among these was Pass Christian, were
Montgomery's Hotel served an unforgettable pompano,
lake trout, and red-fish chowder.

But watering places were only one of the many pleasures open to the people of New Orleans. For example,
Hall portrays in detail a "king's ball" of the type generally held on sugar plantations once the cane was ground.
He was invited to participate in one of these and so is able
to give us a close-up account.

And that is what Hall mostly does. He wanders around the city (indoors and out), observes carefully, and relates his impressions. Since he wandered a lot and saw a lot, we learn a lot. Hall pictures at length, for example, how sure the people were about their levees, totally confident that they would not be flooded and treating the idea of any sizable deluge from the river as a "humourous absurdity." But Hall sees that the real miracle was not that one heard of only a few crevasses, but that there weren't perpetual ones. He then describes a crevasse and the ways used to close one. Had Hall remained in New Orleans a brief time longer he would have seen the great flood of 1849, one of the worst in the city's history and one which would destroy that careless confidence. He does mention that flood in later pages.

An entire chapter is devoted to "Captain Ric's Epithalamium a la Charivari," in which Hall discourses at length about the city's famous "Sheet Iron Band," led by Captain Ric. To get the most from this chapter we must go back a bit and realize that the charivari in New Orleans was an old tradition. We find one mentioned for Madame Don-Andre Almonaster sometime in March, 1804.

Usually the charivari occurred whenever a pair of opposites got married. A bemused New Orleans newspaperman described such unions in 1834 as those of "a very young man to an elderly woman, or au contraire; or when a very rich man marries a very poor girl, or au contraire; or when a fine looking man marries a hard-featured woman, who is very wealthy, and is blessed with carroty locks, cross-eyes, freckled skin, turnip nose, [bad] teeth—and suspected of an evil tongue." Whenever such a marriage was to take place and word of this got around, a crowd would gather, bringing with it every kind of noisemaker from pots and pans to horns and kettles, gongs, cowbells and so on. It was sometimes called a cowbellion.

The participants dressed in all sorts of bizarre costumes, and the gruesome serenade continued until some stipulated amount of money was handed over. Each refusal or day of delay caused the demanded sum to grow larger. When collected, the fund was set aside for some worthy charity, frequently the orphans of New Orleans, and the serenade ceased. Thus the aforementioned Madame Don-Andre was compelled to hand over "three thousand dollars in solid coin," according to a knowing contemporary. The whole sum was then given to the city orphans. Governor William C. C. Claiborne put the sum at a less impressive one thousand dollars, but in either case it was a worthy gift to the poor.

The custom never abated and by 1838 had reached such dimensions that, as the *Picayune* put it: "For the last two nights we have had it on a grand scale with horns, kettles, gongs, cow-bells, &c. About ten o'clock last evening there were from three to four thousand amateurs in front of the bridegroom's brick mansion and such music mortal ear never listened to before." The demand was a donation of one thousand dollars to go to the orphans.

Most likely this serenade was organized and directed

by Captain Ric, or Ricardo, as he was sometimes called. Leader of the famous Sheet Iron Band, Ric was already the acknowledged king of the New Orleans charivari as early as 1834. The moment any unequal match was scheduled, one city newspaper reported, then immediately "Captain Ricardo, for years the head, heart, and spirit of the celebrated 'Sheet Iron Band' issues his proclamation and blows his horn." Almost by magic hundreds would assemble at the designated place and then march to the home of the newly married couple. If the demanded bribe of from one to a thousand dollars was not met at once, the raucous serenade began.

And it was well to pay up immediately, for "Ric never presses his claim courteously *twice* the same night; no he blandly bows himself out, and at a signal the whole 'Sheet Iron Band' sounds the 'alarum of refusal.' And then such a din, such a 'noise and confusion,' such rattling of dry bones, blowing of horns and conchs, sounding of gongs and trumpets and rattles, and beating of drums." If the couple held out, Captain Ric would "now demand (for he requests but once)" generally double the amount first asked. And once started this way the awful noise continued night after night until the couple either fled for parts unknown or paid the tribute.

As soon as the money was paid, the New Orleans scribe wrote, it was "the very next day faithfully delivered to the superintendent of the asylum, and the amount received is faithfully chronicled in the city papers. Many thousands of dollars have been added to this most charitable institution by the exertions and eccentricities of the amiable, kind, and good-hearted Ricardo."

Toward the end of 1837 the *Picayune* reported a "regular Cowbellion" marching up Camp Street around 9 P.M., "with all sorts of rattle-traps and instruments, from tin pails to stage horns, and from cowbells to iron hoops." There was the one reported by the *Picayune* in March, 1838, as occurring "on a grand scale." Again in May of that year the players of pots and pan gathered in the name of charity. In reporting these events the *Picayune* thought it would be well to explain the New Orleans charivari for the benefit of "some of our distant readers [who] are perhaps not aware of the existence of such a musical entertainment." If such were indeed the case, the *Picayune*'s own accounts may have begun piercing that void and spreading awareness of the noisy New Orleans custom. For towards the end of that year there came news of a concert in Boston in which a "Sheet Iron Band" offered a program "that would beat our cowbellions, calathumpians, and charivaris all to pieces." But the *Picayune* didn't really mean that—it was merely being gracious. Neither Boston nor any other place had Captain Ric.

It was six years later, in 1846, that Oakey Hall first encountered the New Orleans charivari as organized and conducted by Captain Ric and his Sheet Iron Band. Hall calls Ric a "Czar of Music; an Autocrat of noise," and he proceeds to give us an extended picture of the man himself, whom Hall had encountered on several occasions. He probes and tells us who Captain Ric actually was, what his profession was, what his motives were, how he organized his charivaris, who participated, and what his efforts produced for charity. The result is the fullest and best account of this New Orleans institution as it was in the 1840s, including a particular and very amusing charivari. No account of this social and charitable amusement can be complete without it.

No commentator on the city of New Orleans could possibly omit a trip on the Mexican Gulf Railroad to the plains of Chalmette, where the Americans had won such a resounding victory over the British invaders. That battle was only a little over thirty years past when Hall visited the site. He was therefore able to meet and speak with veterans of the battle. In particular, he took with him to the field a veteran whose running commentary provides a firsthand view by one who was there.

Since Hall remained a newspaperman at heart, as well as a lawyer, his comments on the press in New Orleans are especially valuable. Up to the time of his writing, Hall says, literature in New Orleans "has been a great deal like a moss rose in a plantation of Canada thistles." But he finds hope of better things to come in two newspapers, the *Picayune* and the *Delta*, which were giving "tone to the Crescent City press." Hall then proceeds to discuss point by point the innovations and qualities that set the *Picayune* apart. The result is a valuable picture of the state of journalism in New Orleans in the 1840s. Hall tells us of the early efforts of "Phazma" and "Straws" (actually the brothers Jim and Mat Fields) along with George W. Kendall and F. A. Lumsden as they sought to improve the paper by injecting humor into previously staid subjects. Hall turns next to the *Delta* and compares it with the *Picayune*. Finally, the *Commercial Bulletin* is accorded similar treatment, but with less extensive coverage. The *Bulletin* was probably included only because Hall had written for that paper as well as for the *Delta*.

Hall wrote a final piece on his voyage up the Mississippi to Louisville when he departed New Orleans in the fall of 1848 to return to New York. If one compares the writing here with that of the opening chapter, Hall's development as an observer and reporter during the two years spent on these pieces is notable.

Hall might well have ended his book here, but in 1850, as he was putting it together in New York, he received word of the deaths of Sergeant S. Prentiss in July, 1850, and of John McDonogh in October, 1850. For the first he wrote an article for *Literary World*, which he reprinted in the book as an extended footnote to Chapter XI, "A Visit to the Opera," presumably because Prentiss was often seen there. For McDonogh, Hall added a long appendix in which he gave his own perceptions along with what he had heard of this fascinating figure. It is a welcome addition to the literature on the recluse philanthropist.

And that leads us to Hall's one glaring omission. How he could have lived in New Orleans in the 1840s and been as observant as he was without ever turning his attention to slavery is a puzzle. The word *slave* appears but twice in the entire book and then only in passing. One feels an acute sense of loss that Hall did not see fit to focus his powers of observation on such an important and inescapable fact of life in the Crescent City. We can only speculate that perhaps because he read law with John Slidell and became a close friend of Judah P. Benjamin, he was sympathetic to their views. Even so, it is hard to see how he could avoid writing something on what he must have seen. Urban slavery was vastly different from plantation slavery, and there was no better place to observe and study this difference than in New Orleans. How much more we could see today through the eyes of Hall had he only chosen to open them to the "peculiar institution" while he was there.

Hall thought that this book would probably be his last literary appearance, since he had returned to New York to enter law and politics. He did carry out those intentions in a spectacular way, becoming the mayor of New York during the heyday of Boss Tweed and Tammany Hall. He built a large law practice and successfully acted as his own defense attorney when he was indicted for complicity in the Tweed Ring scandals. But he never stopped writing: essays, sketches, newspaper articles, personal experiences, and even plays. For three years (1879–1882) he was city editor of the New York *World*. The list of writings he left at his death in 1898 is long, but the title which has worn the best is *The Manhattaner in New Orleans*.

THE MANHATTANER IN NEW ORLEANS

THE

MANHATTANER

IN

NEW ORLEANS;

OR,

PHASES OF "CRESCENT CITY" LIFE.

BY A. OAKEY HALL.

New York:
J. S. REDFIELD, CLINTON HALL.
NEW ORLEANS: J. C. MORGAN.
1851.

TO

SAMUEL W. OAKEY, Esq.,

OF NEW ORLEANS.

MY DEAR SIR:—

IF to prepare a Dedication of the ephemera comprised in the ensuing pages be not too unpardonable presumption, I pray You to accept, at my hands, these Sketches of the City, whose steadfast citizen and public-spirited advocate, through evil and through good report, You have been for over thirty years; of the city which You have beheld, during this period, quadruple in size, and whose streets, now burdened with the treasures of metropolitan wealth, were, at Your first arrival, but the avenues of disagreeable approach to the swamps of the Faubourg St. Marie.

That You may live for many happy years to

watch this city of your adoption continually
increase in commercial prosperity and metropolitan importance, surrounded by the social enjoy-
ments that You so much adorn, and that You so
heartily relish, is the earnest prayer of the

AUTHOR.

HUDSON-STREET, ST. JOHN'S PARK,
  New York City, Oct., 1850.

INTRODUCTION.

THE majority of the sketches in this volume were written at New Orleans, in the years 1846 and 1847; and have appeared from time to time in the " *Literary World.*" The kind consideration they received from many readers, and their endorsement by many gazettes in this country and Great Britain, have induced their collection, after much revision and some additions, for publication. They are presented with the hope that they may afford brief reference to many phases of life in the South-western Metropolis, about which there is little known in other sections of the country. And, as thus presented, are probably the last literary appearance of their writer, who, in the pursuit of a congenial profession, which tolerates no rival pursuit, will have little leisure for additional labors in the fields of Belles Lettres.

TABLE OF CONTENTS.

X.

XI.

XII.

XIII.

XIV.

XV.

THE MANHATTANER

IN

NEW ORLEANS.

I.

GETTING TO NEW ORLEANS.

THE "Father of waters"—the tortuous and elastic Mississippi River—possesses a most unpoetical mouth. No one can deny that. But its distorted shape—almost suggestive of dental wrenches and forceps—may be excused when considering the number of watery relations who avail themselves of his good nature to escape from forests, swamps, and dreary solitudes thousands of miles in the heart of the North American Continent.

And the surrounding features of the *landscape* (daring the wrath of Academicians Durand and Doughty, for thus designating the portions of soil at the embouchure of the Mississippi River) are quite calculated to impress new beholders with the idea that the aforesaid father of waters beheld his best days, long before La Salle and De Soto left their cards, graven with ingenious steel, on the trees that skirted his banks; and is now altogether

2

in the condition of a river exhausted by burdens
that trade and commerce—relentless giants that
they are—heap upon his back, and steadily increase,
year by year.

I thought the above and much more, as I stood
upon the deck of a packet ship (after the usual
monotonous coast voyage from New York) at the
meeting of the Mississippi with the Mexican Gulf;
and alternately divided my gaze between the clay-
colored water at my side (whose said clay-colored
embrace the blue gulf waves haughtily rejected,
and drew a distinct line of separation to their more
intimate acquaintance,) and the sandy, boggy,
loggy, grassy, and snaggy strips of land that
boasted the name of Balize, (or "Beacon,") and
began the important empire of Plaquemine, in
Franco-American Louisiana—the empire so famous,
not long ago, in newspaper political history.

"An unpromising beginning for New Orleans,"
said I to the pilot who had just ascended the ship's
side, and was preparing her for an "admission to
the bar."

"Our river is very like brandy."—

"Like brandy?"

"Yes—the more one knows of it, the better one
likes it; and you will find it a better ending, when
you reach the Levee to-morrow evening."

A little fat man, whose eye was yet heavy from
sea-sickness, and who, standing by, had heard the
scrap of conversation, was understood to murmur

plethoric satisfaction, with something like a distant allusion to a distant adage, "bad beginning, good ending."

"To-morrow evening, and no wind?"

"We tow up, sir, by yonder steamboat."

"Yonder steamboat! Was the tablespoon shaped piece of timber, decorated with a brace of pipes, half way up whose sides the ingenious helmsman had erected an observatory for a look-out seaward, after stray ships—a steamboat?"

Steamboat!

Shades of Watts and Fulton, in your wanderings through the world, you have beheld many an unpitying adaptation of steam to utilitarianism: but never can you have beheld a more remorseless one, than was exhibited in this aforesaid table-spooned piece of timber, which came "making up to us," and dodging about the ship, like an awkward country lad making advances to his milkmaid sweetheart, when, like our ship on the bar, she hesitates on the top of a stile, thorn and bramble imprisoned, and needing assistance over.

The gallant steam in the boilers seemed conscious it was badly used by the confinement in so unsightly a hulk, for it shrieked, and sobbed, and wailed most piteously, while, spliced to the ship's side, the aforesaid tablespoon commenced an upward voyage.

For twenty hours of day and night—the moon was up during the latter time, fortunately—we steamed through ninety miles of plantations, with their picturesque houses and cabins, and groves of orange-trees (that made one thirsty to look at;) and Lilliputian clumps of cypresses, with pendent, melancholy moss; and by mass meetings of democratic looking logs and snags, where numberless alligators, in sundry oratorical positions, seemed moralizing over the "progress of the age"—the progress of river navigation; until at length we came in sight of the Crescent City.

The sun was setting in a cloudless sky, and saluting the dome of the St. Charles Hotel—that Magog of Inns—and the steeples—alas! how few in number—he lighted up for view a "very extensive range of village," as in days gone by, the Cockney said of Gotham.

On my right, as we steamed up to it, was the broad Levee. On my left, Algiers, a very fitting cognomen for an uncivilized appearing strip of land, sleepily eyeing New Orleans over a mile of muddy water, and walled by flat boats, and hulks of steamboats, in all stages of dilapidation, wrinkled with levee crevasses, and dotted with ship-yards in miniature, until it was wonderful to think how so wafery a piece of ground could retain upon its surface even the small bits of human life, and the collaterals of human business, visible upon it.

A dry dock and an iron foundry were in building. They must sink it, surely, some odd night.

But the City Levee!

In youthful geographical ruminations, I had pictured it a lofty embankment, spurning with haughty look and defiant mien the turbulent assaults of Mississippian floods; or had thought it some species of wall, to which the time-worn structures of Athens and Egypt were mere shells. But here it was a modest commercial plain; pile-built, and earth filled; sloping gradually from the river; variegated as far as the eye could reach—and no small look at that—with cotton bales, and sugar hogsheads, and molasses casks, and corn sacks, in quantities sufficient to gladden the vision of England's Prime Minister, in Ireland's blackest days of distress and famine; and bits of machinery, and ploughs, and oat bags, and hay bales, and staves, and wooden pails, and packages of hemp, and leviathan hogsheads of tobacco, which, to look at, made the stoutest mule shriek in agony, all mixed up, and in worse confusion than the streets about Essex Market, in Gotham, good reader, about moving day, in Sunny May.

Across this levee, stores and warehouses, which hugged the like commodities, in brick and mortar embrace. In front of it, sectarian assemblies of ships, fresh from prow contact with the sparkling waves and foaming billows of all known seas and oceans. Steamboats, too; ungainly water buildings, of three stories in height, with cupolas and domes, and observatories to match, but which, for all their unwieldy looks, could bring their three or four thousand bales of cotton, from half as many miles in the interior, to say nothing of three or four hundred passengers besides. Further down, angry crowds of flat boats, with most picturesque crews: the much talked of flat boats, mere floating grana-ries and coal-yards, secure in their timber fragi-lity.

I had small time for observation. The ship was soon moored; and I was more inclined for a good shore supper than a poetical commercial reverie in a place where one's legs were being perpetually recommended to the notice of experienced sur-geons. Besides, there was small time, in the deep-ening twilight. Deepening, indeed! Once get the sun down, in latitude 30°, and down falls the cur-tain of night, like an act drop on a condemned tra-gedy, or the convincing truth of a bitter criticism, on a young author's comprehension.

"To the St. Charles, av coorse, yer 'onor," said an exile of Erin, in the fancy dress of a cabman, as he lashed on my last trunk; and shutting me up in his vehicle, proceeded to drive me to lodgings.

So busy was I in fancying the surprise of my stomach, when it should once more taste the good cheer of a hotel, that I did not particularly observe, by the dim street lights, the events and scenes of a drive through some of the most singular quarters I had ever beheld, in town, village, or city. I can only recall to mind dioramic and shifting views of avenues of cotton bales; groups of old clo' shops, gaudily set forth with parti-colored handkerchiefs, in number and sizes enough for a regiment of noses; oyster stands, where dirty mouths and flickering tallow candles grinned ghostly satisfaction; coffee and cake stands, in a brace of deserted markets, where negresses and lazy butcher boys were engaged in melodious quarrels quite anti-scriptural in their tone but yet suggestive of the tower of Babel; a dirty park; and streets evidently paved on the principle of five stones to the square yard; all which, at the end of my drive, (drive! odds collar bones and knee-pans, as Bob Acres might have said, had he been my fellow-fare,) sent me to my chamber in the St. Charles Hotel, with hearty thanks that I even jolted through such confusion, worse than confounded, and had no fates behind me to urge a *walk* instead.

II.

Hotel Life in New Orleans.

SET the St. Charles Hotel down in St. Peters-
burg and you would think it a palace. In
Boston, and ten to one you would christen it
college. In London, and it would marvellously
remind you of an exchange.

In New Orleans it is all three. A palace for
creature comforts; a college for the study of human
nature; and an exchange for money and appetite.
But certainly, from the building's exterior, you
would never imagine it a hotel unless waggishly
told it was builded by Barnum, that immortal
guardian of Tom Thumb, and American-godfather
of Jenny Lind. And who, according to divers of
the Connecticut people, is an intuitive architect.

Its builders were very modest men, and constructed it upon an angular piece of ground, hemmed in by lofty stores and narrow streets, and
shadowed by neighboring balconies, and garnished

with oyster saloons, fruit shops, and billiard rooms; and all in such a way that one is as long in finding out its value to a city where fine edifices are as yet exceptions, as was the celebrated financier Jacob B———— (whose pen and purse now control its destinies) in discovering its value for investment.

Some whose critical ideas of architecture have never yet been realized (and probably never will until they go to heaven) are unable to discover the beauty of the building. An imposing look it certainly has when abstracted in the mind's eye, from its neighboring masses of brick and mortar, but in its present site is only a mammoth pearl thrown before swine.

Apropos. Oh City Fathers of New Orleans! clean out the hog-pens around the St. Charles.

But where, in this hotel, can we study human nature?

Imprimis, in the large bar room beneath the grand porch and reception hall, whose subterranean entrance from the pleasant air would impart great satisfaction to a regiment of Goughites, and add new spirits to their watery eloquence. For in it Emperor Appetite and King Alcohol hold their court in a most recherché style. There, of a winter's morning, when the sun is near meridian, or of a winter's evening, when the damp `air or chilly northers without seem to say, "ah, apropos of sandwiches and punch," may be seen hundreds of steady, conscientious lovers of lunches and liquors

2*

going and returning, or clustering by pillar and column in social meriment, listening to the play of knife and fork and the click of spoons in heavy tumblers, and looking at the ruby sparkle in the polished decanters. Hungry men and those athirst getting new appetites. Those fresh from the gombo soup, and the ham, and the punch and julep, rushing back again, unable to be tormented by the mere looking on. Woe be to that deputy barkeeper, who in this retreat is slow of motion, or deficient in energy, or weak in constitution. I tremble to think of the juleps, and punches, and nogs, and soups, and plates of fish, and game, and beef and loaves of bread, that I have seen appear from side doors and vanish (like superior fireworks in old Niblo's of a dry week) among the waiting crowds at the long counter; or of the piles of dimes that each devoted (yet willing in all his agency) barkeeper swept into the little holes to nestle in boxes, and—for aught ˚you or I know, reader—in barrels below.

These crowds appear and disappear day by day, relentlessly eating and drinking their way (lunch-wise) into the early summer. Then the bar boys breathe less short; and punches and soup from a quick consumption get into a decline. Hot water is uncalled for. Juleps and iced ale are in demand until the sunny hours of August, when Yellow Jack comes into town, and the room echoes to the tread of some score or so, whom death nor disease can frighten from the worship of the appetite; or who, secure by acclimation, over their clinking glasses or ice ringing goblets laugh at the passing terrors of the "grim conqueror."

The crowds of last winter!—where are they?

"'Tis well we've so large a country," thought I, asking myself the above question one September day as, just myself through the yellow fever ordeal, I stood in the room. One barkeeper then looked sorrowfully over the air-tenanted area before him, and winked despondingly as he thought of last winter; and of Tom this and Harry that and Ned the other, who were now over the Alleghanies, far away; trout fishing in New England, or polka dancing in Saratoga, or flirting at Newport. A theatre bill of the St. Charles, three months old—one of the last night of the past season, and as yellow as though sick with the fever—hung mournfully on a side wall; an old steamboat card, its no less sorrowful neighbor, and an old shipping list, hard by, hanging to their rusty tacks, with the tenacity of autumn leaves on hickory boughs.

But the bar-room below is a trifle!

Turn to the left in the centre room above, about the hour of three on a January afternoon.

The door opens. A hum of voices and a clash of knives and forks and spoons salute you stunningly. What is the occasion? A gala day? A public dinner?

You. see frantic waiters dashing round, going and coming—darting here—darting there; provisions everywhere for an army, surely.

Nothing but the gentlemen's *ordinary* of the hotel! The feeding room of two or three hundred individual bachelors and exiled married ones, who *call* New Orleans their *home* for five or six months in each year, and for the rest possess an undefined position in the world.

Among them although, a few old stagers to whom Mudge and Wilson (worthy hosts, I would you knew them, reader) are fathers and mothers, and nothing else.

Dinner over, the inner and the outer porches, and the pavement, fifteen feet below, are peopled as if by magic, with a crowd, whose toothpicks well accord in poetry of motion with the eyes gleaming so satisfiedly above. What! this large toothpicking crowd escaped from the ordinary just left? Why not? Very true, there are some five and forty eating houses just about; and eat at a restaurant, and pick your teeth on hotel steps, is a stale Boston joke.

Or it is a winter's evening, and in the ladies' drawing room flash beams of beauty, and gas, and jewels.

The weekly soirée of the establishment.

We have seen the bachelor lodgers in their eating, and drinking, and toothpicking ways of life; behold now the ladies with their husbands, brothers, lovers, and a few friends from the outside city. Marvellous collection! The blonde from New England, and the southern planter's son; the brunette from Georgia or Alabama, or interior parish of Louisiana; and the male representative of Western trade, or Eastern manufactures, or British mercantile snobbishness, dancing amicably vis-à-vis in the monotonous, untiring quadrille, or now whirling in the waltz—the giddy waltz, of course, after the usual phraseology; or in that mysteriously born dance, the Polka, of which an American bard long since despondingly asked:

> Oh, Polka, Polka! pray how come you so,
> I've asked ten dandies, and the ten don't know.

Here, too, is modest beauty from Ohio (papa in the pork trade;) there a dashing belle, whose altars at Saratoga and the Sulphur-Springs are yet warm with sacrifices of her last summer admirers (her third winter at New Orleans, and no husband yet.) In yonder corner a red-cheeked, blue-eyed miss from New England (her grandparents snugly in bed the while, in the old homestead, and little dreaming of the—to them—degenerate conduct of their descendant.) Or here a proud Edith Dombey, from Louisville ('tis a city of proud women nowa-days, shade of Daniel Boone,) a fascinating flirt from Baltimore; or the bewildered milliner-mar-tyred daughter of an interior planter. Every state with its peculiar beauty in the room. And the shears and needles of your Boston, Manhattan,

Philadelphia, Charleston, and country tailor recognisable in the dress coats sprinkled all about the room;—black dots, that they are, on a snow white gauze and satin landscape.

There will be music, dancing, nonsense, eating, and flirting, until three o'clock in the morning, and——the same things for three or four months thereafter; but the July sun will shine unrebuked through the window shades, and find this chamber of beauty—this audience room of hotel aristocracy —as tenantless as the bar below.

Although this same hotel was chiselled, and trowelled, and painted, and decorated, and peopled by the genii of Yankee utilitarianism, there lingers about it a deal of romantic interest; and would it could interest in its behalf the pen of a Leigh Hunt, (think of the St. Charles figuring in the Indicator, or a new series of "Men, Women and Books,") or a second Laman Blanchard worthily to embody, in eloquence of essay, truthfulness of sketch, and beauty of diction, confessions of life and character, startling and instructive. For with the latter its every room and vestibule is rife. The very left behind forgotten trunks, piled in a store-room to the bar hard by, could tell a thousand wondrous tales. From yonder window has cast many a stranger his last look upon busy life, and lain down on his pillow to die; thoughts of his far off home and expecting friends making doubly painful the last bitter hour. In this or that room

the gambler lodger has laid his plots, or woven his
web of cunning, which were to ruin and ensnare
those for whom parental solicitude were vainly
expended.   These halls and corridors are full of
echoes, and thronged with shadows; echoes of
mirth; echoes of sorrow; shadows of human life;
their original essence and substance, part of the
past, and perhaps an injunction for the present, to
remember.

III.

HOTEL LIFE IN NEW ORLEANS.—RESTAURANTS AND LITERATURE AT MORGAN'S.

A S if the St. Charles was not a sufficient offering to the Gog and Magog of eating and drinking, whose court, as held in New Orleans, is not to be despised or lightly treated—a plainer and more modestly demeaned hotel has been erected on an opposite corner, in its appearance much like the famous "Holt's" of Fulton street, and which takes its name, "The Verandah," from the semi-orential and semi-French gallery that runs around the second story, and is supported by iron pillars heading skyward from the side walk.

The Verandah prides itself upon its cosiness. The snugness of its exterior and the comfort of its inn-door life possess peculiar attractions for families. And there is about it altogether a home look and a home feeling as pleasing as it is novel for New Orleans.

The Verandah has an aristocratic cousin in the St. Louis Hotel, which stands in the elder portion of the city and boasts a French baptism. It possesses quite the air of an Italian ducal palace. And the idea is nursed by the view of dirty streets, and dirty faces, and dirty moustaches all about; and by the cafés and casinos sprinkled around within convenient hailing. Tall buildings and smoky chimneys hedge it in; and one will almost break his neck in the narrow street it fronts endeavoring to catch a glimpse or two of its façade and summit. Magnificent intention and gigantic plan stood its godfathers at its first christening, and, like not a few godfathers, were remarkably injudicious. So it will long remain a part of the unwanted wealth of the city; the headquarters of Creole loaferism, (understand, good reader, that Creole is a word signifying "native," and applies to all kinds of men and things indigenous to New Orleans.) It is warmly and spiritedly supported at lunch time and o' evenings; and its rotunda (a gloomy looking place with its echoes and marble pavements surrendered to groaning deputy sheriffs and ranting auctioneers, who cry their sales in alternate French and English with musical tone, as if a plethoric sow should change every other grunt for a sostenuto falsetto note,) one may hear nosed more French than a nervous headache could withstand in a minute's time.

And, for my humble self, I shall never hear of

the St. Louis Hotel without thinking of dirty shirts and moustaches.

So much for the three first-class hotels!

If any one dislike their look, a lodging can be chosen almost anywhere. Furnished rooms and cafés elbow each other wistfully; and bachelor bread-toasters, coffee-boilers, and the like, are soon picked up from neighboring shops.

Somebody has called New Orleans "the boarding house of these United States." Certes, its every tenth house has furnished rooms or appliances for travelling appetites; nests for the human swallow-birds of passage, who make wintry flights to southern altars of Mammon, and sacrifice the delights and pleasures of home in their native places, that they may work for the yellow metal, and obey "honest Iago's" advice, of "putting money in their purse."

As for promiscuous appetite—the appetite which dealeth in quantity not quality, and snaps up anything, that is "filling at the price"—this will find a café or restaurateur on every block; from one which tolerably emulates its counterpart in world-renowned Paris, at a charge of from fifty cents to a dollar and a half for anything approaching an appetite-satisfier, down through various grades of chop, and à la Sweeny eating dens, to the more plebeian oyster-stand and bar-room counter, where, for a modest dime, the hungry stomach may procure an hour's "stay of proceedings."

I can never forget those marvellous two blocks upon St. Charles street, running from the great hotel towards Lafayette Square. For in no other metropolis has greater vexation been brought to brick and mortar, lath and timber, than we find endured by these two blocks, which, from newborn autumn until dying spring, are redolent of oysters and lunches, juleps and punches; or filled with the echoes of falling tenpins and clicking billiard balls.

Have you fortitude to imagine five and forty houses (all in a row, like the fiddlers of the immortal King Cole) set apart for the express behoof of hoosiers and strangers, who, for lack of better employment, eat and drink and smoke away the daylight and the night?

In their centre, not long since, an association of philanthropic capitalists erected a large Exchange, and solemnly dedicated it to purposes of literature and commercial discussion. But in a year from its philanthropic christening, its spacious ante-chamber had become a drinking shop—the bar, some fifty feet in length, and backed by splendid pier-glasses that cast unrebuked reflections upon gaping mouths, and watery eyes, and ruby noses—above were lodging rooms, from which were ruthlessly driven the hoping spirits that had shiveringly come to regenerate the neighborhood.

But yet literature (of a kind) and drinking rooms touch noses in cosy friendship in New Orleans.

The same building which screens post-office mysteries from the vulgar gaze, protects an extensive
depôt for periodicals, and by its side a bar. Within
this building every day, much-abused post-office
clerks, and over-praised bar-boys, and the good
natured, smiling Morgan, vie with each other in
their assiduity to customers.

Few who visit New Orleans fail of knowing
"Morgan;" a man who long since took the infec-
tion of good humor, and makes it contagious
everywhere he goes. Turn into the Exchange
building from Royal street. In the passage way
you pass the dirty man whose idiosyncrasy seems
to lie in the manufacture and sale of buckskin
purses and suspenders, upon whose wares press the
crowd that patronize newspaper literature through
the postman's little hole, behind which heaps of
pennies darken the atmosphere; and the negro
girl, with her flowers and cakes, and who is always
knitting (what it is you can't unravel;) and the
cigar man—all of whom blockade the entrance to
the post-office and bar, (on which latter you turn
your back to drop a letter or to call your box
number,) and make the passage in and out, a thing
to be talked over for a day afterwards; and
through a pushing crowd (if 'tis steamer day, and
every day is steamer day just now;) and holding
your nose against the seductive savor of mint and
lemons; and shutting your eyes to forlorn marine
views and portraits hanging all about (you'd think

for sale, only there is no lunatic asylum in the vicinity;) after which you dodge through a smoky door, and there you are at "Morgan's." Straight before you on a table all the papers of the age— English, Irish, French and Spanish; City, and New York; the Mammoth weeklies, too; "Punch" nudging the "Nation; "Yankee Doodle" grinning over the "Western Continent;" the "Sun" shining benignantly on the "Literary World," and the "Baptist Advocate" looking black-typed sermons for "Sunday Times." By their side a wooden box, into which merrily drop the silver coin, as the crowds go by. Further on, the modern novels, not to be counted, but for measurement by the yard. Around a little railed in corner, the magazines. Hard by them the yellow-covered literature of the day—translations from the French, no way improved in morals by their transition from sparkling Parisian to slow-coach English. In sundry corners, cob-web penned and shadow-darkened, stand in military array editions of annuals and school-books. Leaning over the various counters a listless crowd. A nervous lady is dipping into "Godey," and her hat ribbons instinctively fly out as she unrolls the fashion plate. A medical student almost makes your heart to bleed, so brow-knittingly he pores over the "Lancet." An English cotton-broker is chuckling over the toryism of "Blackwood;" his Irish neighbor scratching his head enthusiastically over the "Dublin Nation."

Divers Hoosiers, deeply absorbed in the pages of some such tale as " The Eagle of Popocatapetl, or the Cave of Blue Ruin," with covers quite " sicklied o'er with the pale cast of thought." Penniless loungers reading by the hour, and criticising half audibly as they go, as independent as if good-natured Morgan, whose arm trembles with the wrappings and tyings up it suffers minute by minute, had their reading's worth all snugly nestled in his stout money-box, and they with an honorable receipt upon their day's conscience.

If any association of disappointed literati should dare the abduction of Morgan, what indignation meetings they would hold about New Orleans !

IV.

The Calcutta of America.

NEW ORLEANS is decidedly entitled to be
called the Calcutta of America.

Thwarted enterprise, baffled endeavor, youthful
hope, desperate plannings, all emigrate to its precincts to battle with fate, or to court fortune; to
amass wealth, and if living after the " gold hunt is
over," to return *home* to spend it. Few and far
between are they who cultivate within it a home
feeling, or who fall in love with it at first sight; or
who, by long residence, become growingly enam-
ored of its charms.

" Work, work, work," is the unceasing cry.
Every one appears in fear lest daylight should
cheat him of a dollar. Except among the Creoles
—the aborigines of the place—a man of leisure is a
wonder. On 'change; on street corner; at the dinner-table; between the acts at opera and theatre;

in the drawing-room; at the ball or soirée; in the
sleeping apartments; stocks, cotton, sugar, and
money are the liveliest topics.

Taste in the fine arts and love of the belles-lettres have hitherto fallen victims to the smell of
trade, and money that fills the in-door and out-
door atmospheres. And yet, amid all the discour-
agements of the place, there are many patient
spirits at work preparing leaven for a future New
Orleans literary loaf.

The loaf will be very good, no doubt, but the
baker, whoever he may be, will go into bank-
ruptcy!*

I remember that one morning in May, I astonished my night-cap by doffing it a few minutes before sunrise, and making an ascent to the dome of
St. Charles.

The city's pulse was at a low beat, and its stream
of life in the many street arteries as sluggish as the
blood of an apoplectic. The wind from the Gulf
came in gentle puffs, toying gracefully at times
with the flag that waved above me in compliment
to the presence of some solitary lodgers in the

---

* These sentences were written some years back. As capital
has accumulated in New Orleans greater attention is being paid to
the matters of belles-lettres and the arts. The common school
system is working admirably; and the Municipal library bids fair,
in ten years, to be *the* library of the South. De Bows "Commercial Review" is published in New Orleans, and is a magazine dis-
playing much literary ability and sectional research.

rooms below.   A dusky cloud swung to and fro
like a dropsical balloon above the swamp on my
right; and the slightest possible fog was rising
from the Mississippi that, far as my eye could
reach, "went on in its winding way" like a
huge slimy serpent creeping upon the face of the
earth.   I was above the entire city with a very extensive drop of the eye upon chimneys and roofs—
very extensive when I thought that half the range
a ten years back were not summoned into existence by the magic wave of trowel and plummet.

Across the river at "Gretna" (no place for runaway lovers, reader, although blacksmiths are
plentiful thereabouts, and forgery a common crime,)
a tinkling factory bell was lazily performing its
office; perhaps reluctantly, if it had in remem-
brance the sleepy eyes its sound was calling to
consciousness.   A tow-boat in the river some miles
below the city was puffing its way to the city,
hugging in its monster grasp a brace of thousand-
tonned ships.   Above, one of the crack Louisville
packet-steamers came by the groves of ghostly
cypresses as proud and imperious in bearing as a
mettled racehorse upon the turf which his hoofs
had successfully known time and again.

The sun was next beheld hovering over the
Gulf, maturing an audacious dash at the many
eastward windows of the city.   A faint hum began
to be heard; the groans of the city for the coming
of another day of trial; increasing every minute:

" From field suburban rolled the early cart,
    As slept the revel so awoke the mart."

First the rattle of the milk wagons. Next the
dashing cabs from the early mail-boat that was
taking its morning smoke behind the swamp.
Now and then the clatter of hoofs upon the pavement told that some shoulder-bent book-keeper
was taking his morning equestrian exercise, and,
sportsmanlike, thinking of the race the "ledger"
daily gave him. The ponderous dray shook the
houses as it thundered toward the Levee, drowning
even the stentorian voice of its driver "boy" im-
provising upon "Mary Blane" or "the Rose of
Alabama."

The hum soon became a roar. The caldron of
New Orleans commerce was again upon the boil,
and as I looked around I could scarcely keep from
moralizing and extemporizing an essay upon the
eternal American theme of the country's destiny.
Here was a city half increased in fifteen years;
what would it be in —— but the hotel gong warned
me to a breakfast toilette, and I left the essay in its
primitive and useful chaos.

But there is perpetually upon exhibition this
panorama of trade at which I took my ante-break-
fast glance from the St. Charles dome; and I have
often seen a stranger from interior wilds gazing
upon it with astonishment and admiration; and
perhaps with awe.

His station may have been before the custom-

house, which in the hollow of the crescent-shaped
turn the Mississippi has, commands the view of
miles. Before him is stretched the plain of wood
and earth—before alluded to—the Levee; under
which not long ago rolled the treacherous colored
flood now some couple of hundred feet encroached
upon the opposing shore to make amends for its
this side subtraction. A wilderness of ships and
steamboats skirt it—if 'tis early morning. If but
one short hour after sun-rise, the decks and wharfs
are all astir, processions of loaded drays are going
by, three mules at length before and twelve feet
of neck-breaking timber behind, their continuous
stringing making street-crossing hazardous and
quite a work of skill. Thousands of hogsheads,
bales, and bags and packages crowd and jostle
and hedge each other in. Adown the riverward
streets flow rapid streams of human heads and
legs, whose escape from an entanglement is quite
a disappointment; sailors; stevedores; steamboat
hands; clerks; planters; wealthy merchants too;
running to and fro with divers projects in their
head, and all the solutions to end in the *quod erat
demonstrandum* of money. A million dollars could
not buy the articles of traffic taken in at one
glance; articles of traffic that before twenty-four
hours have gone by will all have disappeared—
their place supplied by different lots and newer
samples. Above the tornado noise and bustle can
be plainly heard the hailing among water craft;

the bell-ringings of arriving and outgoing steamboats, which leave and come with an amusing air
of nonchalant accustomedness—butting headwise
to their Levee berths like a sick man at sea endeavoring to climb to bed. These dissolving views
have been seen for years, and will be seen for
years to come.

And there are many guides to tell you all
about it.

"How do you like the city?" inquires an old
resident. While you hesitate for an answer, himself replies:

"Excellently, of course; fine commercial advantages, eh?—the store-house of the Mississippi
Valley—great destiny ahead."

Fine commercial advantages! so everybody
thinks. And everybody in that opinion is right.

The strongest backward endeavor of black destiny could not retard the prosperity of New Orleans.* Nature had her eye upon the outlet of
the Mississippi long before she invited her sister
Art to form a co-partnership in the way of com-
pleting a grand commercial emporium. The waters
of a score of mighty rivers mingle with the waves
that dash the Levee and float down treasures of

---

* Perhaps the enthusiasm of former years has stated this too
strongly. It is becoming evident to every practical thinker in
New Orleans, that her citizens must build a railroad running north-
ward to the Ohio River. There is great danger of a diversion of
western trade by the means of eastern railways, canals, et cetera.

produce and wealth increasing every year. New Orleans is the market for the products of three climates.

And the traveller in New Orleans must believe all this the very day he lands. For heaven preserve him from the old button-holders of the city who upon some rainy day, when, as the price lists say, "out-door operations are at a stand," will decoy him into a corner and prose over New Orleans in the "Past" and in the "Future;" who will tell him how much its commerce increased thirty years back; how the French retarded it with their dancing-master ways of business, and how the Yankees gave it gigantic pushes; how ten years ago the ground now forming the dray-worried streets of the Second Municipality was but a swamp and a place for croakers of another kind than those who big with stocks and exchanges "bull and bear" in Camp-street; how what now is swamp, in ten years hence will break out scrofulaly with brick and mortar dwellings.

Let one instanter make up his mind that the city is to be the greatest in the world. If so it turn out to be, in his grey-haired time of life he has but to look knowingly and say, "I knew it all along." If it does not he may keep mum; and no matter.

V.

A Peep Into the Exchange.

LET us stroll to the exchange, some evening, where oddly enough, but in strict accordance with the iron sway of utility, 'change time is at early candle-light; for daylight is too precious in New Orleans to be wasted in a lounging talk.

Above the bar and post-office (the former out of sight, you'd think, but no, looked down upon through a wide cut-out in the floor) are the talking, smoking, reading-rooms of the merchants. By twilight they begin to fill. The dozen chess-tables in a small recess are early taken up—a crowd stand round for observation and remark; and calculations are begun, and checking done by men who have calculated and checked all day to some purpose. By and by the sand upon the floor is scraped about like the strings of a violin when innocent "thirteen" is learning Paddy Carey. Knots of

readers stand around the bulletin boards and by
the tables, where the gazettes of all the States are
lying. But everywhere a talking, money night-
mared crowd. Yonder is the cotton broker, with
the fluctuations of the market for a ten years past
all penciled on his face; his brain divided into
sections like the columns of a balance sheet, for
dollars and cents, or farthing's rise and farthing's
fall, whose life is only nursed on from year to year,
and saved from shipwreck on the grinding sands
of anxious care by the summer trip he makes to
England, or to France, or to a Northern State.
Near him is a sugar broker, fat with perpetual
tasting of the sweets of life, whose jolly phiz, and
merry laugh, and careless talk are fine offsets for
the troubled look of his neighbor "in the cotton
line." In one corner the banking agent, whose
principles are in London or Paris, (their correspondence a nightmare in the dreams of lazy post-
masters,) chatting familiarly with the jolly planter
who has just doffed his hat in return to the obse-
quious bow of a passing factor. In another corner a sallow-faced man, versed in the tobacco
mysteries (you may tell it by the nervous twitching
of his face) is figuring estimates for the London
market. His neighbor in the flour line has his
thoughts in Boston, and on memory's wings is
dozing around its built up cow-paths for a sale.
Some are English—you can tell them by their
rosy look, the oddity of their hat, the starch of

their collar, and the hang of the coat. The French you know by their volubility and gesture. Others are Germans—as they read or talk, no sparkle of the eye or change of features indicates their thoughts. Some are Yankees; there is a sharpness in their eye, like the feel of a Bostonian east wind on Cambridge bridge. Some are from Gotham; they carry themselves with an unmistakable air of superiority and independence; and although merchants now, and family men, they feed on the important feelings of their clerkship days, and the savor of the old Pine and Wall-street times hangs around them still. Some from Philadelphia; their gestures are all right angles, and invisible parallelograms are on the floor wherever they walk. And you could work out algebraically the number of pins in their well adjusted neck-cloth. Some from —— everywhere.

If there is ever to be a Congress of nations, let it be held in New Orleans; there will be no mileage for delegates. Of all the crowd, perhaps not one calls the city his home, from birth or choice. Faces are here upon whom the Exchange gaslights have shone for many a winter; faces, too, that next year you will look in vain to find. All intent on speculation and accumulation, working for them all the day, dreaming of them by night.

So it is in every country more or less—be sure of that. But yet you may search the world over to find the science of money-making reduced to such perfection, and become of such an all-engrossing influence as in New Orleans.

But if the denizens of the Crescent City work for money in the daylight, gas and candles see it freely spent. The clerk is at his bowling, or his billiards, or in theatre parquet. The mechanic at the circus, or the minor ball. The beauty and fashion of the city throng the concert-room, or besiege Donizetti and Halevy from latticed boxes in the Opera Français. The evening is the reaction of the day; the prolonging of the money-fever.

Here and there are quiet drawing-rooms, from the breasts of whose inmates, and from whose tranquil firesides, at which domestic love is ever a chaste presiding goddess, the demons of Mammon have not wholly driven away home pleasures wherein the quiet soul which has escaped the fascinations and seductions of the perfidious sirens of fashion's train in the world without, may gratefully share.

These are the oases in the desert of New Orleans life. Happy they who are as fortunate as myself in finding them.

3*

VI.

The Municipalities—Their Architecture and Promenades.

STATISTICS of municipal law and policy are not very amusing or attractive, we know; but to a pair of Manhattan eyes, accustomed in the time of spring tides to bethink him of certain Aldermanic routines, and at all times from Brooklyn heights or Trinity steeple, to regard New York as one beautiful and systematic whole, it is very odd to strain the vision over details of the legal divisions and municipal governmental-plottings prevalent in the Crescent City. But in these days of guide-books, gazetteers, and news, none need to be more than reminded that New Orleans is divided into three apparent cities, each of which, as far as legislation goes, attends to its own business; protects with due care its own respective Aldermanic gods; dirties or cleans its own causeways; puts out

its own fires with its own reservoirs; fines its own
rowdies; and puts itself into debt without the vulgar interference of neighbors. The electors of
each part only meet in harmony once in two years
to choose a supervising council (general vestrymen
of the parish) and a Mayor, whose gracious prerog-
ative it is to pour occasionally upon the troubled
waters of fraternal discord the oil of municipal expediency!

New Orleans has a Mayor! But the people
seem sadly afraid of him, and have made his office
very much like that of King Alfourite's prime minister in Planché's burletta of Fortunio—

> ———you'll learn your duty in a minute,
> 'Tis but to hold a purse;

but there the analogy ends, for the purse in the
play (agreeable to the rhyme) had "nothin' in it,"
while the Mayor of New Orleans, on his seven
thousand a year, can study the mysteries of turtle,
regardless of expense.

One section of New Orleans, the First Municipality, is the old city, left to the tender mercies of the
French and Creole population; narrow, dark, and
dirty (meaning either their city or the people.)
One, in the Second Municipality, the new city;
with here a little of Boston, there a trifle of New
York, and some of Philadelphia, with something of
the *rus in urbe* so charmingly common to New
England towns. The third section a species of
half village, half city, (unmistakable in its French

Faubourg look,) is given over to the tender mercies of the Dutch and Irish, and the usual accompaniments of flaxen-polled babies and flaxen-tailed pigs.

A foreign tourist has observed that the democratic character of American institutions is sufficiently attested by our houses and edifices. Each property owner possesses his peculiar ideas of architecture, and independently carries them into effect. In no city is the latter more striking or absurder than in these three sections of New Orleans. The architectural tastes of every nation have been consulted: perhaps in some part of them a Tartan or Japanese sojourner might feel at home. On one block will stand a row of buildings that might have been transplanted bodily from Marseilles or Lyons; their chambers filled with revolutionary memories. Upon another block a dozen straggling dwellings remind one of Spain or Mexico—a pair of dark eyes and a head of most picturesquely uncombed hair here and there beheld wonderfully assisting the illusion. In one part, a down easter has faithfully copied in wood and plaster his old homestead on the Kennebec or Penobscot Rivers. In another, Kentucky taste (so independent and yet so good humored) has attempted to satisfy the longings of everybody by working up a dozen architectural plans into one uncongenial whole, erecting a sort of brick and timber monster that— should they behold it—would drive "Downing" or

" Thomas and Son" crazy. Piazzas, verandahs, and Knickerbocker "stoeps" corner one another vigilantly. Dropsical chimneys and lean smoke vents harass each other tormentingly. Skylights and dormer-windows ogle one another gapingly and squintingly.

And my word for it, with my eye full open to the city roofs, the cats of New Orleans have fine flirtations and mystical gambols o'nights.

The original city fathers of New Orleans (original they certainly were) must have been born poets and have afterwards deeply studied the classics. They named the streets in the mood in which their subjects erected dwellings; consulting everything and everybody. At the christenings, mythology and history, conceit and whimsicality stood sponsors; French Dukes and Princes were given up to immortality upon corner signs; and " Chartres," " Conti," " Burgundy," and " Condé" will never be forgotten in New Orleans so long as black paint and iron spikes exist. In the same manner the various saints came in for their share of fame. So did many sinners. The early governors were not forgotten, as Carondelet, Villeré, and Claiborne-streets attest. The Muses and the Graces contributed their refinement to the swamp infested districts of the Faubourg St. Marie. Oh ye Gotham cavillers at the utilitarianism that has numbered and lettered your streets and avenues, what would you say to Nayades and Dryades and

Bacchus-street (in the latter a Temperance Hall)
which run into Felicity-road, and are intersected
by Calliope and Clio and Erato and Thalia-streets,
begging pardon for the omission of Melpomene,
(who has a "raging canawl" in her midst, a standing theme for "Picayune" jokes,) or Terpsichore,
whose very curb-stones quadrille it as the oozing
mud beneath wells up and down on thawing
wintry mornings. When I add that the Indians,
and the sires of the Revolution, and the living
statesmen, were also remembered, I have said
enough to convince the most skeptical that the
original fathers of New Orleans were born poets.

And any one who has merely loafed about the
city will readily grant my assertion, that Phono-
graphy has before it a wonderful task to translate
unto Hoosier comprehension, at a first sight, the
mystical names that spectre-fy beholders at every
street-corner.

Descending from buildings and street-names, we
jump to the pavement and trottoirs. And they are
worthy of notice if only to appease the grumblings
of fastidious pedestrians who, on the polished flags
of Gotham or Philadelphia, are for ever fretting at
the wretched municipal economy of bad pavements.
Would that Dr. Alcott and Boss Richards, (whose
boots and shoes will ever stand in mammoth letters
on the pages of Knickerbocker history, kicking
aside all ungenerous sarcasm,) or time-honored ex-
street commissioner Ewen, were in New Orleans

to behold *its paves and trottoirs*. How the former would prate of consumptions! The second of cork-soles ; perhaps latterly of gutta percha. And the last named of McAdam and Russ. Certes, as these sidewalks now are, bunion doctors and corn eradicators carry on a thriving trade, and fearlessly paint up their names everywhere. Full three-fourths of the walks are of ill-burnt brick, which, on loose slimy soil, are treacherous feet supporters. Even on sunny days the layers of mud are ten times worse in pedestrian effect than Gothamic or Bostonian deposits of snow and ice; particularly this in the Creole portions of the city, where the inhabitants seem tainted with hydrophobia, and grow spasmodic at the view of water. Each alternate brick is a dandy trap. Down goes the unsuspecting foot, and up flies on face and trowsers a treacherous fluid, for which mud or slush were too generous names. To what end, alas! are boots blackened, or patent leather and white stockings sported in New Orleans in the winter-time ?

"Remember this, my boy," said an English friend as he bade me adieu on the Levee, "the authorities of New Orleans are in league with the cabmen and shoemakers."

Who knows!

I have often thought with pity of the New Orleans-ward exiled belles of Broadway, and Washington, and Chestnut-streets, so used to the peculiar delights of their own promenades. In some rash

moment, when fate presented to their eyes the
dissolving view of a young gentleman in a tender
and impassioned attitude, whispering vows of love,
they forgot, while speaking the tremulous "yes,"
that their ardent lover was a New Orleans exile;
and little thought what a fate awaited their gaiter
boots and their bridal attire, when they shipped
themselves to the Crescent City. For trade in the
latter has put shopping on short commons, and its
extent is bounded by some half dozen narrow, ill-
paved streets.

And yet, on sunnydays in autumn and winter,
rich bonnets and feathers and dresses dare all the
perils of box-encumbered, omnibuses-bespattered
trottoirs, to plan and carry out the usual feminine
attacks upon the articles of dry-goods and millinery
so temptingly, tastefully, and liberally displayed
within the circuit of these half dozen blocks.
Alas! that the fairy pedestrians of Chartres and
Royal-streets should be so little noticed, and so
remorselessly nudged by the passing crowds of
men, whom the task-masters of "business" are
urging on from corner to corner, from store to
store, and from post-office, custom-house, and banks,
to and fro.

No! New Orleans has no promenade. The
existence of one as a lounge would be an anomaly.
And the magician who *could* give her one would
never dare the attempt. There are but few street
dandies to be moved in the matter; a mere sprink-

ling among the scions of the lazy, luxurious *Creole* race.   *Quel dommage!* when a coat from first class drapers stands your purse in fifty dollars, and your trowsers are netted upon the tailor's books at fifteen or twenty.

VII.

CLIMATE IN NEW ORLEANS.

THE climate of New Orleans is a piece of mosaic-work among the climates of the earth; and it defies the ingenuity of classification or consistency of description. The wind and the sun in New Orleans are "to one thing constant never," but always in warfare. It would seem, upon thinking upon it, that every emigrant from the different latitudes, zones, and tropics of this terrestrial ball, brought with him thitherward a bit of his own home climate by way of a souvenir; and that with the collected bits an involuntary joint-stock climate company has gone into operation; which said company, however often it liquidates, always recovers again, and continues operations more vigorously than ever.

At New Orleans you may often walk beneath orange-trees whose tempting fruit and fragrant

foliage wave aggravatingly in a chilling blast,
while your own body corporate is wrapped in a
great coat alarmingly suggestive of a Rocky
Mountain clothing store. Or you may often put
a red nose (more frosty than jolly) to a rose
that grows in an open garden in the wintry air;
whilst the violets blooming at your feet alongside
the flower-bed you pass shiveringly, agree admirably in the colour with your blue lips.   The "bon-
vivants" of the Picayune newspaper enjoy their
vaunted salad and green peas by a blazing February fire, obligingly remembering the while the
health of him of the Boston Post, to whom is
reserved the discontented luxury of reading the
account of the gastronomical doings of his southern contemporaries.   The iced juleps imbibed
upon one December evening are succeeded by the
grateful hot punches of the succeeding evening;
indeed often the two may sit cosily upon the same
sideboard to induce the exposure of individual
thermometric feeling. And Boreas and the Sala-
mander hold levees upon alternate days.

The months move along in diversified procession; fantastic as the reviews of your village parade days. January, who comes in with merry
voice, and who in some latitudes is as dignified
and haughty as a Russian prince, is at New Orleans as capricious and teasing as a village flirt:
now demanding your overshoes and now your
pumps; now asking your Blucher trowsers, and

next bringing your nankeens from their last autumn resting place in your chamber armoire. February is spiteful, and whether she bite them or burn them, hangs doggedly at your ears. March is the month for the trial of patience; you nose a balmy day for a week before you feel its breezes upon your temples; and sometimes try in vain for the same period of time to forget a damp muggy day, whose reminiscences hang about your system like some goading wrong. But April! ah, a glorious month; and true to her poetic character. January had his ducks: fat, and juicy, delicious every way, whether you stewed them or roasted them or smothered them in pastry for a game pie; but April with her pompano (a fish of an Indian name) draws ducks from the memory of your palate as soothingly as Parmly draws a pet tooth from its much loved socket. May is like many a lady whom you and I, reader, have often met; she is cool on first acquaintance, (perhaps she thinks her sister, April, has been too familiar with her gentle goodness,) but gradually warms to your affection. June is the month for your amateur in meteorology, the month for consultations with the thermometer broiling on your piazza. If it hang high, and you, like myself, are a short man, you must needs eye the mercury on tiptoe, for it's up, up among the doubling twenties. And yet after walking in the sun a bit, to return and find the mercury raging at only 90°, a feeling of disappointment has you fast, that so much heat should come from an "only 90° day." I have known some silly enough to quarrel with the heat measurer, and get themselves where they would have the mercury, at fever heat.

When July comes, New Orleans takes breath. Her streets are relieved by the absence of some thousands of her winter population, who in their disappearing, work problems in numeration; at first going by units; then by tens; next by hundreds; and if under the favor of the Board of Health an epidemic get a public announcement, the leaving is by thousands. At ten o'clock of a July morning the sun's rays drop upon the city with a power as if the atmosphere was all filled with concave lenses of which New Orleans was the focus. Then the crossing Canal-street (a leviathan of a causeway in its breath) becomes a labor worthy the reputation of the fire-king. Grass which grew prolifically upon the pavements when they had ceased to ring with the continuous clatter of business heels, has turned yellow and sere. Old residents assume an attire quite the thing for a troupe of genteel model artists; and brave the heat in loosely flowing trowsers, with bust as vestless, and throat as stockless as the bust and throat of your sailor dandy. Unlucky cits attempt their first summer-walk with a step and cast of countenance betraying a mind preyed upon by anxiety; some with umbrellas raised (heat shielders;) others walking leisurely along, endeavoring to derive some passing benefit from every little shadow cast by balconies and lamp posts upon the sun's reflected path. The thermometer is sulky; so are the vexed Ganymedes at the soda fountains (Gottschalk, thou prince of druggists, a passing tribute to your carbon;) the drawers of the gaseous liquid momently showing signs of giving out. The day draws languidly to a close; the sun retires from an Italian sky; and long before the evening gun has boomed from the Place des Armes, there springs from the Gulf a delicious breeze which is elysianlike to breathe. Then how the ice cream saloons resound with clattering spoons. St. Charles-street is a garden of mint you'd think, to snuff its atmosphere, although at all the bars the worshipers unto Bacchus are "few and far between" compared with their number a month or two back when ale and cocktails "were the cheese and nothin' else." The parlors of the permanents open to the Caribee-scented breezes; and the frontward piazzas, and the sidewalks even, assume by the aid of chairs and muslin dresses a decidedly social appearance.

August and September are like James's novels —continuations of what immediately preceded them. October polishes up and oils the hinges of the city gates for Nevember to open and admit the returning exiles, who by December have fairly settled down for another season of varied business and pleasure.

The summer weather of New Orleans can show heat, it is true; but paradoxical as it may seem, it has its charms beside. An "old inhabitant" once expressed his eloquent surprise in this wise:— "When we have the finest weather the people all go out of town; where of all the atmospheres breathed enjoyingly by mortal man can you find one more agreeable than that around us of a July evening?"

"Ah! a July *evening!*"

"True, the day is hot from nine to three."

"Hot! A furnace is a kitchen-oven to Canal-street."

"The remedy is easy; stay indoors till night; or if you must pedestrianize, a half pound umbrella will see you through. And even should business call you out, the Gulf-ward wafted evening breeze will make you quite forget the morning."

The "old inhabitant" was right upon one point. *If* one could only get over the morning heat, the weather is delightful. Often for weeks and weeks scarcely a cloud obscures the brilliancy of the blue canopy through which the sun moves in dignified splendor; or a haze deadens the pleasant glimmerings of the "sentinel stars" upon the quiet night enveloped city. It is in the midst of this peculiar weather, however, that "yellow Jack" so briskly drives his death-dealing chariot. And many an unacclimated sojourner has the summer climate lured to destruction. I have often walked through the streets of an August evening, knowing that scarcely an house which I passed but sheltered patients sick with yellow fever; and wondered where in an atmosphere so balmy, and so soothing to body and mind, lurked the invisible but certain spirit of disease.

Your quiet man with a fine bump of mirthfulness under the favor of Fowler and Wells's digits, enjoys with infinite zest the beholding a fat negro of a July day, and again in January, when the north wind takes a long leap from Baffin's Bay, and wanders up and down the streets of New Orleans. In July, perchance at luncheon time, he may be seen at the door of some cotton press stretched full length upon a bale directly in the sun, snoring away with a diapason truly musical; and if ever the terms "basking in the sun" be capable of correct and telling application, they will find that application in the attitude of the sleeping Ethiopian. Of a January frosty day he is bone and sinew only, all his flesh has paid a tribute to the summary exactions of Johannas Fraust, that merry enemy of your Knickerbocker pipe-smoker in days of yore, and who during the past quarter century takes occasional lodgings in southern latitudes.

And you have never seen a fire hugged until

you behold a violet lipped Creole before a blazing grate of Pittsburg coal.   When he snuffs the frost of a " now and then" evening, even his beloved Opera at the Orleans Theatre cannot tempt him to his loge.

4

VIII.

Rain and Mosquitoes.

MY word for it, that if Professor Espy would take a front room on the second floor of any frame house in Marais-street, in the First Municipality of New Orleans, and live within it six months; or hire an office near the corner of Poydras and St. Charles-streets, within a minute's hail of Sol. Smith's box-office or the cracked trumpet of the itinerating circus opposite; he would acquire a lasting disgust of rain water, and leaving his theory of winds, clouds, and storms, betake himself to shingle-whittling, or any other Yankee recreation which is as soothing to troubled nerves.

I have been upon the Catskills when the roof of the Mountain-House reverberated with the peltings of the rain, and when my spasmodic dreams were crowded by floating visions of drowning men and images of diluvian arks. I have worn out several

umbrellas in my day; and overshoe-shod I have
paddled the causeways of various cities; and so
seen something of rain. But I never realized the
capacity of the clouds for water until "going
through a course" of the wet season in New Orleans. When there was little squeamishness, or
modesty, or gentlemanly consideration in the rain-
drops. When the latter rarely gave due and generous notice of intention to commence action.
When small glimpses of hope for an early cessa-
tion during progress were afforded. When the
rain was now dogged, obstinate and persevering;
and now the rapidly succeeding showers charged
the earth like reserve after reserve of cavalry in a
battle.

The soil of the Crescent City, in the driest time
of the seasons, is filled with humidity (and this to
its utmost capacity, at two feet from the surface ;)
and under favor of these aforementioned showers,
soon overflows. Shunning the river, the choking
gutters send their burdens swamp-ward, littering
the angles of pavement with clumps of cotton and
wool, heads of barrels, hogsheads sometimes;
broken paper-boxes, bits of pasteboard, twine and
bagging rope; all which the ever-thirsty swamp
licked, in course of time, into its capacious maw.

If you are a stranger in the city, and the clouds
have liberally dispensed their favors all the night;
and all unconscious to yourself the monotony of
the falling rain has beguiled you into a late nap,

and you arise at ten o'clock to view the prospect without, and then " to breakfast with what appetite you may," you have queer sights to look at. And queerer ones, if business or curiosity draw you out.

Pedestrians are standing on divers corners in a dreadful state of uncertainty, looking gloomily from their boots to the surging floods before them; now and then consulting watches, making feints to jump, and balking; until urged on by the still more dreadful visions of protested bills, undunned accounts, and lost bargains, "accoutred as they were plunging in." Astonished eastern men gazing from office windows, and turning to their Bibles (if any they have) for statistics respecting Noah's ark. Piano strumming misses in the by-streets are executing "Home, sweet Home" (how soothingly the melody vibrates the out-door air.) Valiant bank runners and collecting clerks wading (apparently unconcerned) through Canal-street, jostling nicely-poised umbrellas, or skilfully navigating them (aerial machines) about the tall heads and wide-brimmed, hats (the latter sometimes knocked off with provoking ease,) and low balconies, and projecting signs, and nuisances of awning posts. Here and there fat men who are victims of circumstance are seen with large umbrellas —canopies, morelike, of silk and whalebone—in narrow streets, caught and brought hard up by a pile of bricks or a stack of boxes. The unemployed cab-horses everywhere are in melancholy attitudes winking and blinking, martyr-like from behind their cosy headstalls, and smoking vigorously the passers-by. The drivers with oilskin capes, (as if one needed to be so cruelly reminded of the state of the weather,) standing under dripping corners, and dexterously dividing the pouring streams about them with their whip lashes ; or peering, aggravatingly, from the back seats of their vehicles through the leathern curtains.

Anon, the earth would seem tired of " staying herself with flagons," and as if by telegraphic direction the heavens would suspend their rain-drops. Then the air would become chilly, and the ascending moisture hang in fog as low as the lamp posts ; the chimney-tops, and the St. Charles' Dome, and the tops of the flag-staffs skulk in a misty obscurity.

And again, when brisk allusions to that clearing-up shower had circulated through the city, the rain would once more descend in torrents, and set at defiance all deductions and calculations of meteorology.

I never take up a New Orleans newspaper, and read from the price current of the day the words, " in consequence of the weather yesterday out-door operations were suspended, and sales of produce were limited," but I know directly that the said " yesterday" was a day like the one above described.

I often roar with laughter, even in my bluish, dumpish moments, at thoughts of a ludicrous scene once witnessed by me, an incident of a rainy day; when as one may well imagine, the slightest incident is worthy of being booked, (for a rarity,) like one of Prince Albert's jokes. The water was six inches deep on the corner of St. Charles and Canal-streets, and my pedestrianism was at a stand still in a fruiterer's shop. Cab-horses were splashing and spattering along like country nags in shallow meadow creeks; and timid clerks in patent leather boots (caught untimely with them on by a bit of deceptive sunshine at early morning) waded shiveringly by, looking grimly at the "Musson granite buildings" opposite, that just as grimly looked back at them. The stands of the fruiterer on the curb (the shelves running from awning post to awning post) were filled with high-priced oranges and watermelons (*sunny* May, by good rights, reader.) A knot of lazy negro boys on the opposite corner showed their white teeth on the black prospect about them, and wistfully eyed the palatable merchandise across the surging currents. Presently a cabman turning the corner, deceived by the overflowing gutter, drove a wheel upon the curb, and with the lurch of his vehicle turned over some shelves of the fruit stand. In a moment the miniature maelstroms and gulf-streams all about had caught in their embraces hundreds of oranges and scores of watermelons, that went floating towards the swamp. The fruiterer was paralysed; an Italian, too, and Monsieur Cabbey within tongue and fist distance! Not so the knot of negro *garçons* opposite. The knot quickly untied and plunged in hot pursuit of the escaping fruit; and with a strict observance of the laws of political economy regulating the division of labor; since no two seized the same melon or clutched the same orange. A group of boys on an upper corner also wished to share the spoils; and a struggle followed their arrival, with a probability of soon testing the swimming qualities of all the party. This aroused the owner of the commodities, fast becoming, in a legal sense, flotsam and jetsam; and the now enraged fruiterer rushed after the predatory bands. But they had two blocks of flooded causeway the start, and much of the spoils was already appropriated. Thinking more of punishment than of his property, he caught an orange at every step and hurled it at the retreating enemy, to the astonishment of quiet lookers-on from drawing room windows, until at last, what with the captures and his own reckless expenditure of ammunition, he was bankrupt in melons and oranges.

The latter, if there is any value in the old saying regarding stolen fruit, were sweet morsels to many a palate in the Faubourgs that night.

Of course, where such a swampy soil and so much rain is found, that eighth plague to modern

Egyptians, the mosquito tribe (insect, and not Indians) are to be discovered without great scrutiny. Your mosquito is a sad drawback in the sunny days and pleasant nights of a New Orleans exile. The mosquito! whose bark is perhaps more disagreeable than his bite.

The month of March in the Crescent City, whether he comes in lamb-like or lion-like, brings mosquitoes, which by April have completely colonized bedrooms, drawing-rooms, and saloons; nay, "all out-doors" besides. And of two classes. One for night duty, one for the tasks of daylight; both equally systematic in all the details of their operations. When twilight deepens, the class that have slept all day in obscure retreats behind curtains, and in wardrobes, and in the shadows of furniture, sally forth and dance about with a noise like the humming of a boarding school of tops. Then is reading a suspended recreation. Old gloves are a treasure. The presence of a veteran cigar-maker is a prize. Fans are a luxury. Woe to that person who becomes immersed in thought, or interested in conversation, or overcome by drowsiness in exposed situations. In ten minutes' time mosquitoes have duly marked him as a rash man; and on the morrow his mirror will become suggestive of small-pox; and his cologne bottle and flesh brush will find active employment in the duties of the toilet.

One retires to rest, and, with as much of the rapidity of lightning as can be employed by nervous fingers, draws his bar of netting and duly tucks it in ; forming a wall secure against the assaults and mining and sapping operations of the whole mosquito army. Behind this he lies until morning, and can sing to his heart's content " Beneath cool shades reposing" with an orchestral accompaniment whose only fault is its monotony.

There is much of science to be displayed in getting beneath this netting of the bed so that none of the hungry swarms accompany you. I found it no bad plan to institute a feigned attack upon one side, thus drawing thitherward every insect in the room ; and then making a rapid march for the other side escape them thence into the snug quarters of your bed. Or taking a corner seat for a few moments as if about to read ; and when the wily insects are beguiled towards you make the same rapid march for the further corner of the bed. Perhaps often there will be a few mosquitoes who have already obtained an entrance, (admitted to the bar under some new constitution and without an examination,) after ingeniously plotting and planing through the daylight like the burglars they are. They must be carefully assassinated, while some good friend without or your body-servant holds the light in assistance of the tedious search that must sometimes supervene before the prey be ensnared. In default of the friend or the body servant, a little experience, and an attentive ear, will make you a sharp-shooter even in the shade of night, as, guided by the humming of the enemy, you track him to execution.

Old jokers will tell you of mosquitoes who contemptuously spurn bars and netting ; and who will crib your bed of straw or even mattress hair, and suck you (julep wise) from without. But this is scan. mag. against the whole insect tribe, and Porter of the " Picayune" should long ago have been assessed in damages for the story.

Cunning and sagacity are eminent characteristics of the mosquitoes of New Orleans. Those who in the daylight most do congregate, know a cane-backed chair a room's length off. They can detect a slight break of leather in your boots as soon as brought within their reach. They are sworn enemies to holes in the elbows or short arm coat-cuffs; or low shoes; or bare necks; or gaping shirt frills. And a man in their company need well examine his hat before tipping his head with it, or combing and brushing of hair will become rather an exercise than a mere duty of the toilet.

But joking and metaphor aside, the mosquitoes of New Orleans deserve a distinct niche in the temple of its history. They are parts and parcels of its population ; coming between the negroes and the mules in nuisance valuation; and far before all men, women, and children in point of numbers. They are differently sized, and differently shaped, and differently armed, and differently aged, and differently educated, according as they are in different sections of the city. The First Municipality possesses its mosquito denizens who have become torpid, sluggish and lazy. Then there are the mosquitoes of the Second Municipality, who are active, energetic, enterprising; who get fat on borrowed capital ; who serve and receipt their own bills; who are always active and vigilant. Some of them are dainty, and associate only with fat people whose nightmares are based upon turtle steaks and oyster pies. Others have a promiscuous appetite, and cling to drayman, hoosier, and banker with equal tenacity. Some are deficient in instinct, and suffer, or die unknown and unregretted in damp corners of closets and on dusty window panes, while their more shrewd and crafty brethren get fat and audacious. Some live through many seasons; seemingly smelling a frosty day twelve hours off, and duly housing in some cast off garment which prudent observation has taught them will not be called into active service; or seeking the friendly aid of a warm chimney corner whither no dust cloth or broom of vigilant housemads may track them. Some have eyes keen as their bills, (these are on the day watch, and are old the moment they come into this breathing world, to judge from the greyness of their moustache and hair,) and will watch from a corner of the room until you are absorbed in reading or writing or in reflection, then making a sudden dash, lance you, take a long pull, (like a thirsty man at an iced ale,) and withdraw to a rumination; whilst you are left to scratch and rub at leisure the small sized mountains raised upon the place of their visitation by the poison left behind. These do not expose themselves to assassination; but are wary and watchful. Speaking *a la militaire*, if you are eyes right, they have left; if you are eyes front, they fall on your rear; if your eyes are all over, they are nowhere. If you strive at any time to clutch or imprison them in the closing palms, you will find that, Macbeth-like, you had but clutched an airy and unsubstantial vision.

Apropos of mosquito diplomatics. A friend of mine with his wife, came to New Orleans for a few days in the month of December, preparatory to steaming across the Gulf to Havanna in the Steamship Alabama, then in the trade. They 'put up' (so the phrase goes for 'lodging' in the South and West) at the St. Charles Hotel; and the first evening of their arrival was spent by me in their company. I left with the promise to come early in the morning for a short tour among the lions.

The water for my breakfast-eggs the following day was quite refractory in bubbling up to boiling point, and I was, therefore, late at the hotel, expecting to find my impetuous friend pedestrianating the gentlemen's parlor in an agony of impatience. But I walked through the various apartments without finding him. "Perhaps he is tired of waiting, and so gone," thought I; "I will inquire."

"Ah, number 25 is in the smoking room, sir—ah stop—No. 25 that was—No. 25 is now No. 30—couldn't stand the click of the billiard balls near him—No. 25 has not come out yet," said the good natured and voluble clerk whose mind was wedded to the now involuntary habit of classing ladies and gentlemen by the rooms they filled.

"Beg pardon sir," said a waiter, "25 had breakfast sent up to them,—beg pardon again sir, but acted very queerly too, and took the trays in themselves through the crack of the door."

"Parbleu," ejaculated I, "they must be sick—let me run up."

"Jack my boy—beg Clara's pardon for looking in; but are you sick," I cried through the keyhole.

"Come in *sans ceremonie*," answered the full-chested voice of my friend. *He* was not sick at all events.

I went in but immediately started back!

"Ha, ha, ha," laughed out my friend as he sat very composedly in his easy chair with his wife opposite, and a very tolerable *debris* of a breakfast on the centre table; "dont be frightened: it's rather amusing than otherwise."

"Now Jack," pouted his usually lively wife, "I'm sure it's a horrid adventure; worse than encounters with African beasts."

I was gazing speechlessly at their countenances,

which from the hair line of the forehead to the point of the chin, looked like bushes full of half ripe black-berries.

"Ha, ha, ha," shouted my friend, "I'll bet a quarter you've the same idea as my wife's maid, who, poor little traitress, has gone off somewhere after merely looking in upon us—I'll bet a quarter he thinks. we're getting the small pox," he continued, turning to his wife who slightly relaxed her pout as the cheerful hilarity of her spouse resounded through the apartment.

"It certainly looks like it," said I.

"We're horrid frights I know," added his wife rather despairingly of tone, "and that's the reason we are not down to breakfast at the ordinary."

"But it aint small-pox," chuckled my friend, "it's—it's—it's *mosquitoes!*"

I took a step or two forward and glanced in at the adjoining bed-room. There was no netting to the bedsteads!

"Why Jack—Clara—my good friends—where is your 'bar;' this is unpardonable neglect from the house; I———"

"There—there; be easy, don't blame the wrong passenger, it's all our own stupidity in not calling for some one to hang it up. Poor unsophisticated Yankees that we are—coming from a place where a mosquito is pinned against a cabinet shelf, by naturalists for a curiosity—what did we know about mosquitoes and netting and all that.; and the thing has been laying on a chair by the bed-side all night. But I must tell you all about it. Hold on a bit, though, for a good 'scratch!' When we first retired we thought there was a curious hum in the air; presently the buzzing came nearer. My wife had the first bite; (as we used to say in our fishing days;) and Clara you know is exces-sively nervous with the very *idea* of bugs in any shape. Soon the truth flashed on us. It was mosquitoes! I got up and struck a light. Clara joined forces and at them we went with slippers and boots. I suppose we killed some hundreds or less—the rascals biting us all the time—when we rather became exhausted. Clara proposed opening the window and driving them out with napkins— a womanish plan you know of de—parlour—ating flies. So we opened the window and slashed about with towels at a vigorous rate. Miscalculating mortals that we were: there was an "army of reserve" waiting outside and in *they* made; and down come the window sash *ex necessitate*. We retired again; and again came the buzzing and the biting. One stout mosquito regularly waylaid me like a highwayman; the light we kept burning and I eyed him for half an hour. Now he would come one side and then dash at the other; then feigned to withdraw only to resume attack. It was doze—buz—bite—thrash—slap—and scratch until day light, and here we are what we are. I suppose we're in for all day? Shall we not frighten everybody and set all the mothers in the streets crazy with the vacination fever ?''

So much for a night of unsophistication with the New Orleans mosquitoes.

So much, I repeat, for rain and mosquitoes in New Orleans. But I advise you, reader, neither on the faith of my representation (true as gospel though they are) nor on those of any one else, to throw either topic in the teeth of your true blooded Crescent citizen.

He rather likes them than otherwise ; and calls them agreeable peculiarities of climate, as your Gothamite speaks of mud, and your Bostonian of zero weather or easterly winds over Cambridgeport bridge.

IX.

Yellow Fever.

DON'T shrug your shoulders, reader, at the heading of these paragraphs; for I am not upon the threshold of any physiological details; I am not commencing a medical treatise which would be valuable in its way to the "London Lancet," or to various Journals of the Faculty which moulder in drug smelling laboratories, or journey with emigrants upon trunk covers; I have no intention of boring the literary world with a diagnosis of the disease which accompanies cholera and plague in the catalogue so often pondered by nervous people. But having had an encounter with "Yellow Jack," I deem it not ungenerous upon my part to say a few things about him; especially as he is at times no unimportant sojourner of the Crescent City.

Not that I know his birth and origin; not that I am in possession of full particulars regarding his nurture or education; not that I am intimately acquainted with his domestic habits; not that I have phrenologized him and discovered his most secret characteristics. Alas! (the interjection is thrown in at the thought of my inability to convert into waste paper the pamphlets which have been published to prove or disprove that the breath of Yellow Jack was infectious and contagious—one or both—and to be shunned like the lepers who shivered in olden time around the wall of Jerusalem) alas! I say, I cannot settle the many questions which have hitherto puzzled the modern disciples of Hippocrates, on this subject; and which have caused as great a disagreement among the members of the faculty as a heavy meat pie at a medical dinner.

Throughout the winter in New Orleans the "fever topic" rather drags in conversational circles. To the "old inhabitants" it is an old story; to the unacclimated it is like allusions to that first promissory note due six months hence which figures on the books of a young tradesman. But when cloaks and thick coats disappear, and pedestrians contemptuously kick about the stray lumps of coal occasionally met with; and the suns of latter May crisp the tops of new carriages, discussions upon the fever are agitated. Will it come this season? Do you stay and weather it? Does Dr. Stone or Dr. Kennedy go to the Virginia springs this summer?—et cetera, ad infinitum, are questions rife everywhere. The yearly members of the Board of Health become characters for ocular interest as they walk about the streets. Their nods and winks and various gestures are scrutinized with great care; and should any of them be suffering under dyspepsia or any other complaint productive of a long face and sour speech, an article on Yellow Fever is sure to get into the Gazettes, either editorially or by favor of some " X. Y. Z," correspondent.

July comes, and perhaps a " case" is announced at the hospital. The very timid have long since left the city; a few fearful swaggerers have remained and now take the alarm. Trunks are being packed everywhere, and the steamboat lists anxiously scanned, when the Secretary of the Board of Health picks out the most humane looking quill in his escrutoire, and says to the public in very readable type the next day, "only sporadic." Ah! sporadic; and the temporary alarm subsides. One, two, three, four, five cases in a day soon occur, but still no more alarm. "They are only sporadic! The Board of Health says so; the sexton's book says so; the sun shines as heartily on the St. Charles' Dome every morning; why should I fear?" cries the shoe-quaking citizen as he sips his morning coffee. Very fine logic all this, but one naturally asks what difference does it make whether one dies sporadically or otherwise!

Perhaps soon the deaths increase, and the Board

of Health are compelled to hang out their newspaper banners with the word epidemic very
conspicuous thereon.   The word is a perfect
sesame.   At its pronunciation, the bar-rooms become almost deserted ; the jolly bank-runners carry
their funds fearlessly under their arms, for the
pickpockets are not to be found ; merchants read
the papers behind their counters, or write letters to
their absent wives ; the clerks, most of them of the
unacclimated, talk over the subject and display
unheard of learning upon matters of medical interest ; the theatres are closed, except, perhaps, the
little National hard by the egg and coffee woman
in the Poydras market; the steamboats at the
Levee may be counted at a glance ; the shipping
look like November forests; the papers are barren
of domestic news; and the arrivals of produce and
of strangers at the hotels are few indeed.   Girod-
street, and Julia-street, and the New Shell road,
and Circus-street, and Rue de Conti are dotted
through the day with hearses and carriages on their
way to the Protestant Yard, or the Cypress Grove,
or the Cemetery of St. Louis.   An ominous looking cart stands at the door of the Charity Hospital.
Physicians' gigs rattle around.   The list of daily
interments head the editorials in each gazette,
as being the most interesting item for home and
interior subscribers.

Any one who after a " hard day's work" of
mental labor in midsummer, has, at an evening

jollification finished three bottles of iced champagne and retired to bed in a badly ventilated apartment; and who can recall the sensations of his mind and body the ensuing day, can well imagine how one feels under an attack of yellow fever. A civil war is raging in the stomach, while the temples and the pulse beat a tatoo for the engagement. The head feels as if filled with molten lead which is burning the eyeballs. The back is like an unhinged door. You seem infatuated with a desire to immortalize yourself by a discovery of perpetual motion, and influenced thereby toss from side to side like a rudderless vessel off the banks of Newfoundland. Daylight becomes a nuisance. The most fascinating of tongues loses its eloquence. Ice is the greatest of luxuries, and you would not sell the bit which covers your eyes (napkin enveloped) for place or money. The blankets around you awaken the most profound disgust for everything woollen. If you are a nervous man you sigh; if a stout man you groan. You can no more sleep than can a man after imbibing six cups of green tea at a New England sociable.

The chances of a patient's recovery vary with the degrees of favor his physician enjoys at the shop of the apothecary. If he have a nephew or a cousin in the drug line, the patient is a dead man from the second day; if he have read Dr. Dickson and Hahnemann, and be a profound thinker upon medical science, supplying its de-

ficiencies, improving its crudities, and softening its
extravagancies by the results of observation, the
patient is, probably, a confirmed convalescent the
fifth day.

A convalescent! The mere being prostrate with
fever—with flushed face, and baked eyeballs, and
stiff back—is the least item in the disease. The
getting well is the most hazardous and the most
annoying. To have a strong craving appetite, but
a frame so weak it trembles with the raising of a
hand; to hear the delicacies of the season cried by
each passing *marchande* fresh, like her stock, from
the St. Mary market, or the environs of Carollton,
but to know they are one and all tabooed articles;
to hear the rattling of knives, and forks, and spoons,
in adjoining rooms at well furnished tables, but be
compelled to supply all the adjuncts by your ex-
cited imagination; to inhale the savor from neighboring kitchens, as your classical memories whisper
of Tantalus: to think of the bills of fare you have
run your eye over in times past, as you find yourself restricted to a wine-glass of ale per diem, fed
out in hourly spoonfuls, and crackers in meat broth
given you as sparingly; these are the real annoy-
ances of the yellow fever.

And this not for a day; but perhaps for a
week; the while, nervous friends and timid relatives fill your gaping mouth, or dim your hungry
eye, with stories of unfortunate convalescents to
whom an untimely apple, or an injudicious beef-

steak, have given the fatal relapse. The man who possesses a small modicum of self-denial will fare very badly in the hands of Yellow Jack, even if he survive the prostration.

That which renders the presence of yellow fever in the city, and its rod of power, as laid upon patient backs, doubly disagreeable, is the almost invariable accompaniment of unsuspiciously fine weather; clear skies, and cooling night breezes. To have a pestilence brooding in the common summer weather of New Orleans, is like suffering a malicious drowning in the waters of Lake George, near its most romantic neighborhoods.

Shortly after my recovery from an early visitation of the pestilential epidemic, it was my wont of pleasant August evenings, to saunter about the city, and examine the various characteristics of summer population; and compare the differences in the look of streets and houses then, with the appearance they wore a few months back. In the Second Municipality, dozens of houses, side by side, would scarcely manifest signs of inmate life. The closed shutters; the dusty pavement; the silent rooms; spoke forcibly of disease and flight. And thus, in walking through St. Charles-street, after passing the beautiful Lafayette Square, (if ever a park within city boundaries preaches eloquently upon the delights of fresh air and greenwood shade, this square, put upon the business vetebræ of the city, discourses thereon most forcibly,) it was something

agreeably noticeable to always find one bijou of a
cottage open, as in the merry spring time; the
parlors, barely above the street level, exposed to the
evening breeze; and cheerful voices and merry
tones, and often pleasing music issuing forth. Occasionally, too, the graceful form of a sprightly girl
sat by the half-curtained window, looking out into
the almost deserted street, while every passer-by
who trod the flag-stones before her, seemed to catch
a lighter step as he went on. Curiosity learned
for me, that she was the daughter of a physician—
motherless, and an only child. Her father, an
adventurer, and an enthusiastic apostle of his art.
He had chosen New Orleans for his abode, leaving
behind a happy home in an eastern State, and many
a sad memory connected with it. He was studying
the progressing epidemic, and his daughter would
not desert him. And there, visited sometimes by
summer residents, they lived on watching the time
when they would have to conduct the usual encounter with disease.

One night I found the shutters closed: they are
gone, I said, to pass away an evening at some
friend's residence. The next night the same deserted look. My thoughts were ominous, and from
a neighbor's servant, I learned that both father and
daughter were ill, "but not badly taken, they
would soon be well."

Both were ill together. They had not thought
of this perhaps. The father counted on ministering

to a sick daughter—his tenderest patient—the daughter hoped to have been a nurse to the father, and so discharge the pious offices of love.

The tale is soon told. The father lived—the daughter died. And the tears start into my eyes even now as I think of the look that father's countenance wore, as a week afterwards I met him slowly walking through a retired street; a blasted future, and a regretful past, clouding the present which should have been so bright. It is but a simple tale from a class whose numbers are too mournfully frequent when the pestilence walketh by night, and wasteth at noonday.

5

X.

Law and Gospel.

IF ever the Shade of Justinian makes a tour to
new countries, it is my humble opinion that he
often visits New Orleans; dodging up and down
the various narrow stairways in Exchange alley
from wide-mouthed Canal-street to the lockjaw
pathway in front of the St. Louis Hotel (said pathway being termed by industrious painters on corner side-boards, "*Rue*",) or skulking in and out
the suspicious-looking, dreary-smelling rooms in
Royal-street; up which and in all which are found
in the shape of lawyers and notaries more zealous
followers of the Civillans than the most enthusiastic
Saxon would like to shake Magna Charta at. It is
my humble opinion also that the said shade takes
a strange delight in climbing the flights of steps
in the sepulchral-looking building adjoining the
Cathedral of St. Louis, wherein justice is homœo-

pathically administered; and in overlooking the
heterogeneous crowds of Americans, Germans,
Frenchmen, Spaniards and a variety of "confounded foreigners" in general, who in the capa-
cities of sheriffs, clerks, advocates, clients, witnesses,
jurors, hangers on, and outsiders, assist in peopling
the court-house of New Orleans, and putting in
solemn motion the treadmills of her code of practice. That the said shade furthermore recreates
himself at times in running his eyes over the
various legal libraries, and in poring over the
various legal briefs in the offices of New Orleans
lawyers. For he sees that on the banks of the
Mississippi in a land his ambitious countrymen
never dreamed of in their proudest days of con-
quering pomp and pride of power, his law and his
legal doctrines flourish in all their original beauty
and vigor; that the sublime teachings of the Pandects school the operations of the most enterprising
commercial community in the New World—and
this an hundred years after Blackstone had stolen
soul and body from Domat the mode of arranging
a legal treatise, which Justinian had himself ori-
ginated, and which has been the pride of your
true-blooded Anglo Saxon lawyer for scores of
years.

There are very few but who are aware that the
doctrines and practice of the civil law are the
principal ingredients in the system of Louisiana
jurisprudence; and that these doctrines, after being

naturalized in French and Spanish courts, were respectably dressed and so placed under the protection of the American flag by the labors of Messrs. Livingston, Derbigny, and Moreau.

And it is somewhat singular that the great majority of legal gentlemen who win the hearts of New Orleans jurymen and soften the prejudices of New Orleans judges, were educated under the common law; and like conscientious proselytes, having their fingers and thumbs knowingly impressed with the pages of Domat, Pothier, Merlin, and Duranton, will find for you in the tables of civil law the origin of trial by jury, of remedial equity, and various other matters of legal lore which are often called the exclusive property of Saxon jurists.

The legal profession has been, and ought always to be, a lucrative one as pursued in New Orleans. Merchants who have traded and leased and speculated under the laws of Massachusetts or New York or Ohio, will very naturally, in the conceit of human knowledge, proceed to contract, while resident in New Orleans, in the same manner as before; and thus proceeding will run upon some snag in the under-currents of Louisiana law and be only saved from total wreck by paying your "humble servant of the bar" a very nice fee by way of salvage. A husband and wife who in their romantic days of courtship and in the honeymoon thought little of property and of the legal rights which they sustained towards each other, remove to the Crescent City and growing older find upon due inquiry that all unconscious to themselves they are partners in what the lawyers call a community of acquests and gains, attended with certain very perplexing and annoying conditions and appurtenances. In short, a citizen in Louisiana soon finds that he must sue and be sued; marry and die; shave and get shaved (á la Wall-street meaning;) sell and bequeath; in a very different manner from that he has been used to in his native town or city. Consequently, as home physicians are always in demand by strangers troubled with the ills that flesh is heir to, so the lawyers of New Orleans will ever remain the walking sticks and golden-headed canes for the citizen in every walk of life. The merchant and the mechanic may never so habituate himself to the legal ways of Louisiana that he can steer his way among the shoals and breakers of commercial currents without consulting a lawyer's chart and compass. The more he tries to study, the worse he will be; for in the matter of civil law the truest application may be made of the old couplet,

> " A little learning is a dangerous thing,
> Drink deep or taste not the Pierian spring."

Therefore, it is not to be expected that so humble a person as " Manhattaner" can expect to successfully bore the reading world with legal disquisitions

upon the topic in hand; or afford it an opportunity
of quizzing rashness and ignorance conjoined.
But I cannot forget the curious scenes I occasionly
saw when in the New Orleans court-house. It fronts
a scraggy-looking square termed the Place des
Armes, with a front and side the classification of
whose architecture would puzzle the most learned
in the art. The Cathedral darkens its entrances
and obscures its windows. Lazy-looking priests
and greasy garçons rub the whitewash from its
base. Apple-women take possession of its lobbies.
Beggars besiege its vault like officers. The rains
from Heaven sport among its rafters. It has everywhere a fatty, ancient smell, which speaks dispar-
agingly of the odor in which justice is held. And
yet in this building (which the poorest Eastern
village would blow up before sundown should it
appear within its precincts) are held from November until July, six courts, whose officers brave
damp and steam enthusiastically and persever-
ingly. You turn out of Condé-street into a narrow
alley aud brushing past a greasy crowd, are soon
within the criminal court, where a judge, perched
in a high box, wrangles hourly with half-crazed
witnesses;—here you behold jurymen, who of
themselves constitute a congress of nations; zealous, full-lunged lawyers; and audacious criminals
ranged in boxes, very much to the satisfaction of
a moustached district attorney and the merry-look-
ing keeper of the Parish jail. You will soon get

sick with staying there, and so entering the next room will see the happiest little judge in all Attorney-dom (here, too, boxed up against the wall like a Connecticut parson in a high-roofed meeting-house,) talking with the lawyers upon the business in hand as familiarly as though he were at his own dinner-table, and they his honored guests.* Opposite, in another dreary room, are entombed the papers of the dead; sitting by a couple of long tables are antiquarian-looking juniors, up to their eyes in all the mysteries of last wills and testaments, inventories of property, and "succession distributions." Climbing a weary flight of stairs, you encounter a perplexing labyrinth of passages. But whichever way you may go (four court rooms and four clerkly offices about) you will see the same boxes against the wall; the same sort of lawyers lounging or running about: some bareheaded (full of business, of course!) some with papers in their hands, grateful to the sight and touch; others (of the junior sort) eying from their airy perches, the jostling crowd below, in hopes to find a runaway witness, or a deceitful defendant; the same collections of books and papers, strangely hid away behind green curtains and red doors; while everywhere a hum of voices rises in discordant chorus, escaping heavenward through a quadrangular court-

---

* This referred to the Hon. E. A. Canon, now deceased, and who, from his name and chivalric impetuosity, was often termed by the punsters " Little Pocket-pistol."

yard, especially built therefor, by the unknown but
humane architect of the dreariest pile of brick and
mortar you have ever run away from with your
fingers in your ears.

But listen! As we are going down the ricketty
stairs, what curious jumbling of voices comes from
one of the rooms! It ceases; and take care of
your head and shoulders, as you turn the angle of
the upper landing; now we are retracing footsteps
—curiosity impelled;—for the whole batch of
Advocates are turning from the room whence proceeded the Babel of tongues, and rushing like mad
into another room. Shall we follow?

But as we go, here's a round-shouldered, red-
faced, clerkly-looking personage, who is walking
the other way, as unconcerned as a stupid snail
in a beautiful garden-plot; we will button-hole
him, and inquire the cause of the tumult.

Manhattaner. Pray, inform us, what is the cause
of these legal gentlemen agitating themselves in so
undignified a manner?

Red-faced Clerk. This is Saturday morning, and
they are fixing their causes.

Manhattaner. Fixing their causes! Explain.

Red-faced Clerk. (Putting on a scornful smile
at querist's ignorance.) All the suits which are at
issue, will be called by the clerk this morning, or,
at least, enough of them, at an average of ten a
day, to take two weeks to try; and the lawyer of
either or both the litigants, as he hears his causes
called, will have to set them for trial.

Leaving the red-faced clerk to his cobwebs and stiff paper, we enter.

The room is crowded. Lawyers of every age, from seventy down to newly-whiskered one-and-twenty, are here jostling around the clerk's desk, who has just commenced with his Muggins *vs.* Flammer, or Cockton *vs.* Trigger, etc. etc.

"Set it," cries one to a certain suit.

"Fix it," adds another, who slightly varies the synonyme of the first expression.

"Put it down," continues a third, improving on the second's arrangement of syntax.

And so the dialogue is continued for fifteen minutes, between clerk and lawyers, until the former considers he has jobbed out for the next fortnight of jurymen and judicial leisure, a quantum of trials: while the judge, in his little box above, sits pairing his nails, or biting a pen, or reading the morning paper. The old lawyers cried, "set it," with an impertinence of equanimity impressive to hear; the juveniles would answer, "fix it," in either pride of having so much of business to answer for, or in the blushing timidity of actively nursing to trial an infant suit—their first litigious child.

The clerk shuts up his book; the lawyers scamper off; the judge turns around to "hear a motion," or "allow a default"; and the under scriveners of the court having looked on for a short time to see the fun, turn into their closet rooms.

5*

Ha! Here comes our red-faced clerkly friend again; he is looking particularly communicative; and I have a further curiosity to know something more of Louisiana practice.

Manhattaner. Is litigation attended here with much formality?

Red-faced Clerk. We do it up here as brown as they do it anywhere.

Here, a blushing young advocate chimes in with his remarks. "Law—ing here, gentlemen, is a treadmill sort of business. We, advocates, (blushing more and more at the word "we,") are one-third of our time in office; another third, in the street, between the office and the court; and the remaining third in these dismal rooms. We (still accenting "we," and pulling up from his breast pocket, the corner of a legal document) draw up our petition in bringing a suit, and lest, on trial, we should have asked too little, we pray for all sorts of legal relief. Bringing our petition down here, the clerk copies it and adds a citation; hands the copy and the citation to the sheriff, who serves it on the defendant; the clerk keeps a minute of what he does in yonder mammoth ledger and of his fees, and the sheriff does the same. When the defendant answers, his lawyer brings his answer to the clerk, and the latter copying it, gives the plaintiff the copy, and makes another entry and another charge. Down come both lawyers, in a Saturday or two thereafter, and cry "set it" and "fix it" as you heard this morning; and so get on for trial as best they may. If we subpœna a witness it is done by writing his name and residence in yonder book; and the clerk and sheriff hunt him up. The "setting" business is a complete lottery. If your case is down foot of a Monday, and not reached, it cannot interfere with Tuesday's parcelled off causes, and over you go for two weeks like a canoe upon the Falls of St. Anthony.

Manhattaner.—Bravo, my worthy! As appears from your statement, clerks and sheriffs are the cog-wheels and levers of your machinery: you supply the fuel; and clients are they who provide the oil for an easy running!

Young Advocate. Then whoever gets beaten here, if his quarrel was about three hundred dollars and over, has a record of all the proceedings made out by the clerk, and again calls the latter and the sheriff to help him to bring his adversary into the opposite room for an appeal. If the beaten party has been fool enough to quarrel about two hundred and ninety-nine dollars or less, he has no redress except to move for a new trial; and then he has his trouble for his pains. But if you are strangers, step into the appeal room; an interesting argument is on by one of our ripest scholars.

I crossed the vestibule and listened to him for half an hour. He was addressing a bench of four judges—an even number, but odd enough when each two happened to disagree. The oldest of them would have passed in Paris for a man of thirty-five; and the youngest was a beau-ish sort of a gentleman, with remarkably fine whiskers, and who, in his after-college days, had killed his brace of banditts in Spain by way of getting up an entertaining volume of travels.

I recognized in the speaker a tall gentleman of commanding appearance whom I had often met walking dignifiedly, and with smiling face, among the busy city groups with cane in hand, which he held rather in compliment to his slightly-furrowed brow and flowing gray hair, than to assist footsteps which had lost none of their juvenile elasticity. His life had been made up of agreeable episodes. Now the admired advocate of his Georgian village; now a member of Congress beloved by all his associates, but little caring for the storms of politics: now a traveller in classic Italy, storing his mind with the lore of the civil law, and amusing the leisure of his severer studies with writing a life of Torquato Tasso: now returning to his native land, settling in New Orleans, and shedding on the severer features of its rough-and-tumble life the chastening influence of his refined taste and classically stored mind. He had for a moment forgotten his classics and his poetry, and that "his life was like the summer rose;" and was deep in the mysteries of the question whether twenty-five bales of cotton belonged to a hook-nosed snuffy

gentleman seated at his side, (and dignified as "my
client" by lips which in their day had smiled upon
admiring throngs in drawing-rooms and saloons,)
or whether they belonged to a broad-backed Ken-
tuckian who was seated by the grate-fire mumbling
some chestnuts.*

---

* Reference is here made to RICHARD HENRY WILDE, who is
well-known to the world of letters as the author of "My Life is like
the Summer Rose," and other melodious lyrics ; and of "The Life
and Imprisonment of Torquato Tasso." He died of yellow fever
in the summer of 1846, leaving unfinished a life of Dante, which
it is to be hoped his eldest son, who inherits his father's love of
Belles Lettres, and who was his companion in Italy, will not suffer to remain in manuscript. The author, at the period of Mr.
Wilde's decease, furnished an obituary notice for the New Orleans
"Commercial Bulletin," from which he extracts the subjoined para-
graph as expressing the concurring sentiment of the entire community :—

"The judge upon the bench, opening his winter term, will have
one less cordial nod to bestow, as he looks around upon the Bar of
New Orleans—the youthful advocate will have one less approving
smile upon his successful efforts—the University of Louisiana will
have one less matured and enthusiastic parent of its promising infancy—the social circle and the festive board, will have one less
admired visitant and honored guest ; and among the hundreds who
have fallen by the pestilence, none will be more sincerely mourned
than the distinguished scholar and amiable gentleman, whose coming, a few years since, all welcomed—whose untimely removal, all
deplore.

In a city like New Orleans, where trade and commerce are the
great monopolizers of the human passions, and the plannings and
the enterprises of their votaries are the almost absorbing business
of life, a man like Mr. WILDE exercised a great humanizing influence. His learning illumined the labyrinths of commercial trans-
actions ; his scholastic graces scattered roses in the retired walks

Religion, in New Orleans, is rather at a discount. But yet public morality (saying nothing of what takes place behind doors, and family screens, and throughout various social circles) is more pure in its character than in any other American city.

Whew! Manhattaner tunes the *lyre* to some purpose, I think I hear exclaimed. Yet this is not overstated.

If Boston, or Philadelphia, could show upon their police books the small number of crimes committed and complaints presented, which appear in the statistics of the Crescent City municipalities, they would be very paradises. Burglars and pick-pockets, when paraded before His Honor of the Criminal Court, are looked upon as for a show by the gaping crowds. The genus loafer is almost

---

of those escaping for a moment from the toils and burdens of the day; he mingled the amenities of life with its cares, and softened its wearied hours with the suggestions and lessons that a refined taste so agreeably prompts—

> Th'envenomed whirlwind o'er the city passed;
>   And, as in forests yields the monarch oak
> At rudest summons of autumnal blast,
>   So did'st thou fall before the whirlwind stroke
> Oh, Poet-Jurist! leaving friends behind
>   Who deeply sorrow thy untimely end;
> And off'ring grief-wove tributes, as they bend
>   Around thy tomb, unto thy master mind!
> Hushed are thy lays; the music of thy tongue
>   Shall ring no more in learning's halls; nor seen
>   The stately form; the winning smile; the mien
> Which charmed the thousand hearts thou dwelt among.
>   And whilst enshrined within those hearts thou'lt be,
>   Each mourner-friend " *will shed a tear for thee.*"

unknown in the natural history of New Orleans;
and cigar smoking juvenile-pittites, fire-rowdies,
and brave insulters of woman, are only heard of
now and then. This in a city where manners and
customs, laws and usages are in a constant transition state; and in whose midst more sectional prejudice, and national jealousy, and individual idiosyncrasies are found than one may hunt up from
the remaining three metropolises of the United
States.

But religion is at a discount. Not a New England town but contains more churches; the theatres
and the opera are open of a Sunday night; bulls
are sometimes baited in the Third Municipality of
a Sunday afternoon; aeronauts ascend from shout-
ing crowds, under the eaves of a well-filled church;
cavalry in active exercise deaden the eloquence of
a popular preacher; firemen in parade jostle returning congregations; infantry are at target practice on the Bayou Road; crowds of merchants
throng the post-office lobbies at noontime. But so
conspicuous is the excellence of the public *morality*, that these things, which appear singular and
reprehensible to a stranger, are little regarded by
the great body of churchmen in the city.

The St. Louis Cathedral is ——

Now, what sort of a thing would you suppose
this cathedral to be? If the word raises in the
reader's mind thoughts of a dome and gothic towers,
and a fretted roof; or of a dim religious light and

solemn grandeur, begetting memories of St. Sophia, or St. Peter's, or (to make a striking descent) of our own Grace Church; you will be much disappointed. The St. Louis Cathedral is a little squat edifice built of brick, covered with mortar; its white naked sides variegated with map-like streaks of green mould, and beautified by innumerable tin gutters, which every rainy day tick and splutter most musically. Place on its side a hook and eye box, and arrange at each end a brace of chess rooks, of the old fashioned pattern (and made before amateurs had " seen the elephant,") and you have a faint idea of what the St. Louis Cathedral is in form. It fronts the Place des Armes, and has its ugliness kept in countenance by the court-house upon its left, and the Municipal Hall upon its right. Its height is that of a common sized three story house; and there hangs a cow-bell in its tower, whose tinkling has brought on a nervous fit for many a judge and juror in the court-rooms hard by, and perhaps lost many a worthy party-litigant his cause.

But for all its ungainliness, you must not utter a syllable against the cathedral, on penalty of excommunication from all Creole society. Built in the latter part of the last century, it possesses the reverence of all the French and Spanish white cravats, and the respect of all their children. It has beheld the raising of the Spanish flag upon the city flag-staff on the square before it; and seen the

French tri-color and the American stars and stripes
successively replace the colors of Spain.   Its aisles
have reverberated with the anthems of praise and
thanksgiving, when, beneath the holy roof, the
Hero of New Orleans and his brave associates of
the 8th of January, 1815, knelt in reverential pos-
ture, while a discomfited enemy, but a hundred
miles distant, were leaving the shores of Louisiana.
It has welcomed the nation's guest, and the friend
of Washington.   Its organ has thundered forth responses to the echoing shouts of a populace hailing
the return from a hostile shore of the " Hero of
Buena Vista."   Its religious rites and ceremonies
are connected with all the prominent events of the
city.

And having such endearing associations allied
to it, one regrets* that these associations could not
perch upon a better appearing edifice, which fronted
upon a better appearing square.

The latter (whose name in French, Place des
Armes, may be freely translated "the beggars' retreat") possesses a very neat iron railing, one or
two respectable aged trees, a hundred or two
blades of grass, a dilapidated fountain, a very
naked flag-staff, and a venerable piece of ordnance,
classically employed every night in giving the negro population the cue for a scamper in-doors.   It

---

* Since these sketches were written, provision has been made
by the pious pew-holders in the St. Louis Cathedral to erect a
more modern and more imposing edifice.

has a water view, and with a judicious expenditure of a few thousand dollars might be made an inviting promenade; it is now but a species of cheap lodging-house for arriving emigrants, drunken sailors, and lazy stevedores; and occasionally the review-ground of the most forlorn looking body of military (their name is "Legion") I have seen outside a New England village upon "training day."

Thus much for reminiscences suggested by thoughts of "Law and Gospel" in New Orleans.

XI.

A VISIT TO THE OPERA.

THE Creole population of New Orleans possess one enjoyment well worth the envying—
an agreeable French opera! None of your mush-
room establishments which exist one day and are de-
funct the next; none of your spasmodic or mongrel
affairs with an English prima donna, and an Irish
tenor, and an Italian basso; none of your half-and-
halfs, whose orchestra is what that piquant specimen
of petticoat energy, Susan Nipper, would term a
" temporary ;" accustomed to perform overtures in
original keys, and with odd variations; or anon to
race after the voice of a common singer between acts,
or " come the pathetic," when injured maidens are
dying in pathless forests, in sky blue silks and
satin slippers; whose choruses are composed of
under bandits, sextons, smugglers, dragoons, and
comedy waiters, who can sing tolerably when the
kettle drum in the cold corner has a stout-eared

maestro with drumsticks of stout hickory; nothing
of the kind. But an opera with a regular standing
array of attachés engaged by (and who sing, too,
without forcing green room quarrels upon the audience) consecutive seasons. The French opera at
New Orleans is, indeed, worth your while; always
good management; always good singing; always
good instrumentation in the orchestra; always an
agreeable, fashionable, and critical audience.

It is a moonlight evening in November. Your
thimbleful of curaçoa upon the top of one of
Moreau's dinners (and you be a bachelor, and your
appetite be not chary of publicity) has made you
a contented and happy man for the time being.
Turning your back upon the melancholy cathedral, the flower-garden behind it, and the grey-
bearded religious enthusiast, who mounts guard in
the vicinity, mumbling prayers from morning until
night; and passing from Royal into Orleans-street,
the billiard balls clicking their fascinating music
in the ear as you pass the confectioner on the corner; twenty or thirty steps bring you to a fox-co-
lored building of plain columned front, before
which stand a row of carriages, and a dozen or two
of laughing, chattering Frenchmen. A brilliant
flash of light, through opening doors, shows you
the cabarets and domino rooms opposite the Orleans Theatre. Entering from the street you are
in a spacious lobby; the appearance of paint and
flooring as fresh as those in Grammercy-Place Man-

sions; a jolly-looking citizen, whom you may see
every day officiating with an amusing affectation
of dignity as crier of a court, takes your tickets,
and turns you over with your place-checks to the
various *loge* directors, who bow you up or down,
in and out, with a grace which, were you in England, or at the North, would suggest the possibi-
lity of there being an unappropriated quarter dollar in your miniature *porte-monnaie*. The parquet
is already filled with critical young Creoles, and
here and there a representative of " Young America," ambitious of connoisseur-ship in music; the
well-brushed heads about, principally belong to
scions of Creole aristocracy; family incomes, or
salaries as genteel clerks, supplying the allowance
of tri-weekly visits to the opera. Behind them,
upon simple benches, are the unwashed patrons of
Auber, Donizetti, and Halevy, who, for a dollar a
head (less by a half the payments from the remainder 'of the audience) have left their ground-floor
lodgings and red-curtained retreats, to gratify their
love of harmony. The *loges* above—some latticed
for privacy, most of them open—are filled with
rich dresses, fairy forms, sparkling eyes, and animated countenances. The Graces flit about from
box to box as though they were not a whit ag-
grieved by having their lodgings on the cold, cold
ground, among the Muses and Dryades of the upper swamp under favor of the Alderman who
named the up-town avenues after them. Every-

where are faces which you know, reflecting a natural and cultivated interest, not the work of artifice, or the promptings of mere fashion. No injudicious encores (to be more explicit, no encores at all—those absurd manifestations of delight, as thoughtless as the man, who, at an aldermanic feast, gormandizes turtle to the detriment of the flavor of the turbot which follows;) no applause worked up at unseemly times; no snobbishness of look, action, or language; no gross inattention.

At the Orleans theatre, when *Lucia*, and *Favorite*, and *Guillaume Tell*, and *Norma*, were being rendered in a style, if not perfect, at least artistic, I have lounged away many an evening with the most satisfied home-feeling imaginable; and have sighed to think that excellence and continuity in English opera should be a matter so unattainable in these United States of America.

But to take you up again in your seat in the stage corner of the parterre—a five-eight view of the cosy and cheerful theatre before your eyes.

Abstracting your attention for a moment from the stage, (excusable in the stranger,) drop your gaze into the parquet. In the third seat from the orchestra, by the side of a tall commanding gentleman, who will deliver a division order to an aide, or, as sheriff of the parish, bow your legal advocate to his deputy; or preside at a public dinner with equal grace and dignity, sits a stout, good-humored gentleman, whose florid face bespeaks a

life of contented ease. He has just left his judicial
box-office some three miles off, and forgetful of the
collective duties of Parish Judge (a historical office now) and Register of conveyances and mort-
gages, is drinking the liquid notes of M'lle. Calve's
Salut à la France, as she triumphantly waves a tri-
colored banner. The music is striking some res-
ponsive chord in his breast. How it heaves; and how
his eye sparkles as the ran-tan-ta-plan of the little
drum sounds in the succeeding march. This florid-
faced stout gentleman, whose law library was dotted with works upon military tactics; who, as judge,
was accustomed to direct the sheriff to charge on
the prisoner, and bring him into court; or to re-
quest the gentlemen of the jury, when the benches
were full, to dress to the right; has, since the time
we observed him in the opera parquet, dusted his
boots in the shell-ploughed streets of Matamoras;
wheeled his charger by the heights of Monterey; tel-
escoped the planted batteries at Vera Cruz; flashed
his brave sword with immortal honor at Contreras,
the hero of the day; timed the entrance of the
American army into the city of Mexico; and was,
for some time, Governor of the new El Dorado on
the Pacific.*

In a loge above him sits the Colossus of the New
Orleans bar; as unmoved by the bright scene
about him, and with a countenance as severely
placid as when his vigorous logic and cool elo-

---

* General Persifor F. Smith.

quence are demolishing with crushing weight the flower-crowned confectionary pyramids of an opponent's argument.* Nearly opposite him sits a keen-eyed, bandit-looking gentleman, who, in various ways, has been the plaything of Fortune; to whose subtle eloquence many a villain owes his unstretched neck; and who, as you catch his reflected countenance in the adjoining mirror, you involuntarily say would be much more likely to feel at home, at some future day, amid the tumultuous debates of a French Chamber of Deputies, than in the United States Senate.† Not far from him is the Van Buren of Southern politicians (we are in the theatre, remember, before political carpenters have builded the Buffalo platform;) the successful lawyer and ex-diplomatist, who, as his adopted State grows older, will yet play a more prominent part in her political history, unless the restless eye and abstracted look of reflection are poor physiognomical interpreters of steady ambition.‡

In the front balcony box sits a short, sunny-faced gentleman, surrounded by a bevy of ladies, (a planter's family, from Natchez in Mississippi, on a metropolitan visit,) who, in the pauses between the acts listen with almost idolatrous admiration to the brilliancy of his conversation; while the occu-

---

* Col. G——s.

† The Hon. P. ——S. ——

‡ An Ex-Minister to Mexico.

pants of boxes, all around, overstep for a moment their accustomed politeness to listen to the sparkling sentences. It is the famous orator of the Southwest. The whilom struggling boy; the schoolmaster; the lawer; the politician; the pride of the social circle; whose name is a household word among his fellow-citizens.*

---

* This has reference to the lamented Seargeant S. Prentiss, who deceased in July, 1850. The writer furnished an article for the " Literary World" on the occasion of his death which he deems not improper to subjoin in this connection :—

THE LATE SERGEANT S. PRENTISS.

To remember the virtues and chronicle the memorial deeds of the dead, who leave their marks on the way-side of the age, is particularly the province of the journalist; a province mournful in its necessity, but grateful in its duty.

Our readers will have observed, in every gazette of the land, appropriate reference to the life of Seargeant S. Prentiss, who died about the first of July last, near Natchez in Mississippi, of a disease which, in the recent war, struck down at their camp-fires warriors of the proudest renown, while they were seemingly in the midst of health, and which, raging in a more rapid type, deprived the nation of the illustrious head, whose loss it is yet deploring in the eloquence and pageantry of woe.

Mr. Prentiss, beyond his accomplishments as lawyer and politician, (which have been so well narrated by the pens of generous friendship,) possessed peculiar claims on the country as a man of literary attainments; and, in this connection, it is most fitting that reference should be made to his decease in the columns of the " Literary World."

He was endowed with genius of uncommon order. There could be no psychological quibbling on this point by any one who knew him in the sparkling domesticity of every-day-life, or heard him in the glowing hours of his eloquence.

They are all among the notable characters of
New Orleans most seen at the opera, and most
eyed between acts by the Lafourche or Attakapas
planter, who, for the gratification of curiosity, ne-

A child of the Republic, without more than ordinary aids to
study and reflection, he grew to be a man of the times. Necessity
nerved his boyhood to exertion; and in the early years of his
life he waged a stern battle with Life. Like the present President of the country he engaged in the ranks of common school
teachers; and like him, too, his talents were observed by the
shrewd eye of experience, and they counselled to the adventurous
paths of the law. Circumstances (the open-sesame of world-
renowned greatness) exposed the treasures of his intellect—for
years of patient toil and observation among men and books had increased the value of natural gifts; the diamonds of the mine were
polished and set.

For years he has been the Cicero of the South. He continued
first in impassioned oratory at the bar; first in the wonderful passages of popular improvisation; first where the brilliant hilarity of
goodfellowship shone at the festive board. An extensive student
of letters, and gifted with an extraordinary memory, to read was
to remember, and to remember was to adorn argument, orations
and sentiment with appropriate classic allusion and graceful quo-
tation.

For a brief time he electrified the legislative halls of the nation;
and the wit, caustic humor, impassioned denunciation, and fervid
reasoning which brightened the yearly prosaics at Washington,
will long be remembered by its habitués as an era in congressional
eloquence. With ancestral home at one end of the Union, and
household gods at another extremity, he travelled to and fro
among various popular and political excitements, in the midst of
which his clarion voice was ever invoked and heard with fresh
delight.

If Mr. Prentiss was unexcelled in the forum, at the bar, and
upon the platform of mass-meetings, he was unequalled in the

glects the commodious wine-saloon up-stairs, from which five minutes before the drop draws up, a musical bell summons to their places the moderate worshippers of Bacchus.

---

exuberance of his social wit, and in the facility with which he adapted thought to occasion.

His versatility of eloquence, and profuseness of wit, were wonderful. To have listened to him is something to remember and talk of as an event. The writer has heard Mr. Prentiss at political gatherings in the meadows of the country, when everyone said, the glorious sun-set skies, and the sublime mountains soaring towards them, the gorgeous landscapes, and delicious breezes, have inspired him; but he has heard him in the crowded and vaporish hall, surrounded with the miasma and gas of city-life, and his freshness of thought, grace of diction, and rapidity of combinations have been equally happy and astonishing. He has heard him in a court-room almost deserted, when he unexpectedly rose to speak, although the occasion was trivial, and the question of slight moment, the room was filled as if by magic at the sound of his voice, and the subject, which in cooler contemplation had seemed dull and vapid, has assumed a dramatic interest. He has heard him when " human life was in debate," and prosecuting officers closed their books, judges forgot their notes, witnesses were suddenly endowed with patience, the dullest juryman brightened with absorbing attention, the prisoner seemed to forget the crisis of his position—all spell-bound by the thrilling words of the orator lawyer. He has heard his winning pathos and silver tones bidding a welcome-home to returned heroes from the bloody ground of Buena Vista, when the wounded seemed to forget their pains, the sick their distresses, and the sound in limb the perils of the past. He has heard him, in the call of charity, relax the tightened purse-strings of the most miserly. He has met him at public dinners, when he bore away from the honored guest the laurels prepared for his temples.

Mr. Prentiss leaves no writings that we know of. Indeed the

I may be prejudiced, but nowhere in this country could I satisfiedly listen to operatic performances after wearing out a brace of coats at the Orleans theatre, and preserving in memory the uniformity of good music there listened to, or the attentive and animated faces there looked upon.

---

use of pen and ink would have only fettered his mind. And few if any, reports of his speeches and sayings are in print; those which have had publication seem tame to those who were present at the first conception.

XII.

PASSING by the *Place des Armes*, and the things
which nudge it on every side, such as fruit
stalls, and rickety cabs driven by picturesque drivers, who form a cosmopolitan gallery of portraits
as they slumber listlessly on their sun-baked leather
seats; and the temporary print galleries around the
iron railing of the park—print galleries that all day
long exhibit, with commendable gratuity, sailors
in large trowsers, on large sheets of paper, bidding
tender adieus to sweethearts in pink gowns, with
balloon sleeves, to say nothing of the various military heroes who are giving, or receiving, or using
swords, the latter occurring oftenest in the vicinity
of heavy white smoke, whose puffy, rolling volume
leads you to query whether or not there be near
by the camping-ground a Dutch ale-house. Pass-

ing all these, I say, and entering Condé-street, (your back to the more modern parts of the city,) you approach the St. Giles of New Orleans. All cities have their St. Giles' precincts, where poverty and vice run races with want and passion, on the different human race-courses, and form pictures for the eloquence of political orators to descant upon, or legislative Solons 'to construct statistical tables from, when that eternal subject, the amelioration of the lower orders, is broached.

But the St. Giles of New Orleans, in its oddity of mixture, and variety of characteristic, will challenge interest with any other city.

Picayune dram-houses (better known among Crescent citizens as cabarets) smoke each other (tobaccowise) at every few steps, whatever way you turn. High brick buildings, filled from ground floors to attics with "apartment lodgers," line the narrow streets about on every side, towards the river, or in the lane-like streets which bear the Mississippi company upon his downward course. Scolding wives, with dishevelled hair and dirty babies, (infant specimens of at least six nations,) compliment themselves, and their acquaintances who may be within ear-shot distance, in language more vigorous and more curious from variety of dialect than choice. Frenchmen are near by, gesticulating; Dutchmen jabbering and making your jaws ache in sympathy within their very sockets; Italians chattering up and down; some, of all these,

in blouses; some in nautical rig; others with
scarcely a truthful claim to habiliment of any sort.
Old clo' shops, of a mouldy smell; junk shops,
where the prevailing smell is of chains and ring-
bolts, (if you have ever been sea-sick, and will pass
them by, you cannot fail to recognize the aptitude
of an illustration else reprehensible,) and shoe shops,
are side by side in amicable intercourse.   Tea-ket-
tles and bananas; bunches of keys, and red or yellow kerchiefs; soap and straw hats; candles of
prodigious length, at times, and prunella gaiters
with polished toes, (quite the thing for a kick-
polite;) marvellously cheap shirts, rainbow hued,
as they lie together; knives and flageolets; and,
not to prolong a catalogue of incongruous articles
of exchange and sale, articles of all possible utility,
are roasting together, store by store, in the sun, or
suffering from the cruel damp, according as may
be the atmosphere of the day about them.   Here,
too, a cobbler has possession of the *trottoir*, and is
hammering away to the march in "*La Fille du
Regiment*," which he heard last Sunday evening at
the Orleans theatre.   There, a tinman's itinerant
furnace and forge are making the curb-stone swell
with indignant heat.   Not far off a brace of "rag
hookers" are disputing the middle of the street with
a couple of quarrelling negro garçons.   Heads
decorated with red, yellow, and flaring cotton 'kerchiefs, brown, black, or sallow faces underneath, are
seen at every window.   There are artisan signs in

French, in numbers enough to give any four blocks in throbbing Broadway the most business-like appearance desirable. Far and near, idleness and industry, dissipation and petty commerce, at their appropriate places of abode, are "holding their own." And as in the midst of all this you stop in the narrow streets and look at the narrow-bricked houses, and have your ears full of strange sounds, you wonder whether you have not bestridden the flying horse, and gone abroad to places Continental: the thought is but for a moment, for you have asked yourself the question fifty times before, on other occasions.

This so termed Crescent City St. Giles is embraced by half a dozen blocks, which also assist the ship-besieged levee in environing the lower markets; and a water-raising engine, which sobs and wheezes by the side of a Bunker Hill Monument of a chimney, as it pumps up water from the river to fill the underground pipes of the First Municipality. You soon get a headache walking around them, and taking a river street, move downward. Still, dram-shops and junk-shops as you go; more flaring goods and shining shoes; oyster-stands now and then, for variety; drays are thundering by; and yet, and yet, as square on square is passed, the million wheels of commerce are turning in a ceaseless round; a cheering round, too, as one thinks of the sum total of bank accounts that everything is momently swelling. You are soon by the side of a compact brown building, fronting on a wide street, (greedy of ground it is, and has a square to itself,) with green grass and shrubbery about it, which look strangely, but gratefully, amid all the dust and smoke about. It comes quite apropos to your last train of thought upon bank accounts, for it is the Branch Mint building; within whose rigid walls are being put into unquestioned shapes the gold and silver, whose power is reflected outside. Postponing a visit of examination until a leisure day, and a brief permit from the polite Superintendent is given for the purpose, you walk around it and turn into Esplanade-street, where your headache grows better, for the noise is not so stunning, and the heavy omnibuses that come lagging by meet with trifling regard, as the thoughts run upon the rattling and rumbling ten squares back. The street is wide, and the sun hot—the scraggy trees upon the grass-plot, that like, as in Canal-street, divide the street into two causeways, only aggravate your appreciation of the fiery atmosphere; and, after a short walk swampward, you turn up a narrow and shadier street. What odd-appearing tenements are met with! Local habitations, surely, possessing some distinctive name! Wide and low; the eaves projecting far over the sidewalk, and the roofs a problem for the skill of a student in geometry. "Whence the misery that lodges here?" is an involuntary ejaculation. Misery! that is very good; glance in at the windows of these houses, as you

6*

pass, and you find rich furniture, and tokens of luxurious comfort, which give an earnest lie to the outside look. These odd-looking tenements are the dwellings of indolent Creoles, who dread staircases and high storied life as a savage dreads a fork for dinner purposes. From the outside, moreover, they have a somnolent look, and after a while you cease to wonder why Creole napping is so frequent and powerful.

Once more swampward! and Circus-street is reached. More width; more scraggy trees; more length of double and broken curb-stone; more hot and dreamy quietude. Here is a park, too, with primitive posts, and consumptive grass. The stranger asks is it hallowed ground? so solemnly still is everything about, from the better class houses bounding it, to the absurd brick and mortar building across it, known as the Calaboose, or prison; and even including the frightful watch-box at the corner, where a smoke-dried Frenchman tinkles a bell, whenever word is brought to him that a fire is burning within the precincts of his watch duty. It is no hallowed ground; and you will believe this well, if you will come on a Sunday afternoon and witness crowds of happy servants shaking the swampy soil with dancing and jumping, or frightening, with the noise of clattering bones, and barrel-headed drumming, the aforesaid bell-ringer from his rickety retreat. So, too, if you will come when a huge tent covers the corner of it, and the noise

of four trombones, and one drum of astounding
power of endurance, that blow and thump all the
beauty out of the Star-spangled Banner (really *executing* it, as promised in the small and dirty typed
bills,) suggests to you that a circus is in full exhibition, whereat occur grand Bedouin entrées of
thirty horses, with candle-faced riders; not to forget the astonishing feats of the brigand, who is
understood to illustrate robber-life in Italy, by
raising himself up and down upon a superannuated
horse, and now and then exploding a pocket-pistol.

Gazing about as you lounge in this park, you
see the tops of some half dozen masts near by.
The Mississippi has as many curious turns as any
nervous woman,—you have already discovered
that; and can it be that after having left it as you
thought a mile behind, you have again come upon
it? This little lane-turn will explain matters; and
it opens to view a fifty feet basin, the termination
of a canal, which extends lazily into Lake Ponchartrain through a sleepy stretch of cypress-cover-
ed swamp. But the canal is under Creole government, and little of bustle is seen about. A few
bales of cotton, a pile or so of lumber, some cut
fire wood, are lying around. A dray stands by
with its boy looking vainly about for some knowing one to inquire of. Vainly, for the skippers and
their crew are quarrelling in a cabaret near by,
over a game of stained dominoes and some *vin or-
dinaire.*

If the commercial prosperity of New Orleans had always depended upon Creole enterprise, I fear me the purchase of Louisiana would not have been so highly lauded as now.

Again pedestrianating upwards through the rear Faubourg of the First Municipality, where the houses are universally low in height, and with projecting eaves, (small array of furniture although,) and walking upon long thick bits of plank, once the gunwales of flatboats, (and the universal sidewalks of New Orleans suburbs, where the little-trodden marshy soil sponges up bricks and stones as though they were grains of sand,) in a few squares' stretch, you will reach the St. Louis Cemetery—Roman Catholic soil. A street intersects it, and brick-walls with ominous-appearing gates hem it in; making a species of fortification, as if the living were in danger of storming a citadel where Death was an inmate!

Various poets have called cemeteries Cities of the Dead; and the expression is forcible applied to those of New Orleans, of which the St. Louis is a representative specimen. Cities of the dead; because from the peculiar moisture of the soil interments are in tombs and oven-like vaults, constructed above ground; the latter in tiers of three and four along the cemetery walls, built of brick and faced with marble, upon which to inscribe the words with which affection consecrates entombed dust. In the area are private tombs constructed

with granite or marble, and varied in form and
finish by taste and worldly circumstance.   To
some, this idea of burial above ground, where each
body has, as it were, a mansion to itself, and which
in most cases is just large enough to hold the
coffin, is revolting. I have heard many a sojourner
say, "Oh, if I die, send me for burial to my northern home,—don't shut me up in those horrid cells."
But to others, the idea that they stood by the side
of one loved well, and conscious that but a foot of
brick and mortar separated a friend's mortality
(which fancy still kept as in life) from their own,
was gratifying. Many of the private tombs of the
St. Louis Cemetery are very costly, but for the
most part more curious in design and execution
than artistic. Some with recesses where private
masses for the dead may be celebrated; with
statues and figures of the saints; and decorated
altars. Many are old and crumbling, and dyed
green with moisture.

When the first day of November comes in, and
the religious index points to it on the calendar as
"All Saints' Day," the St. Louis Cemetery is
thronged with pious devotees of all ages and sexes
—principally females—coming to offer up prayers
at the burial altars of departed relatives, bringing
tapers, and incense, and flowers, to put before
them. It is not a little startling to jostle among
the crowds (for I have seen at least three thousand
people in attendance when the day was sunny,)

walking through avenues of tombs where the dead were laid in rows above each other. To many a tender frame has issued upon such occasions from the damp alleys and causeways, a death warrant which was sealed, delivered, and executed before the expiration of another month. Of the crowd the largest number were mere idle spectators— many, the butterflies of New Orleans, who gaped, wondered, chatted, and talked, as though it were a gala day, and they invited or privileged guests at some great fête. But the humble kneelers heeded them not, and absorbed in their private griefs, thought little of the flippant laugh or stare of curiosity around them. As after such a day I have turned down Toulouse-street, leaving a hum of voices behind me in this "city of the dead," I have thought here is but another witness to the force of the old aphorism, " all men think all men mortal but themselves."

XIII.

WATERING PLACES.

WATER privileges are decidedly abundant in New Orleans. Water over the city a sixth part of the year, under the city, and in front of it, and in its rear all the year. How so little of earth can absorb so much fluid will long remain a problem to muddle the ideas of southern engineers.

Lake Ponchartrain, at the rear, is famous as the place over and through which are conveyed summer after summer, crowds of resident pleasure-seekers in search (can one believe it?) of a *watering place!*

The long line of coast upon this lake and upon its snug neighbor, Lake Borgne—stretching from Louisiana to Florida—is thickly dotted with watering places, whither rush those unfortunate families who belong to the "can't get away club" of the Crescent City; a club so designated in contradis-

tinction to the crowds who at the close of every
winter and spring business make pilgrimages in
search of recreative pleasures to the northerly sections of the Union.

Shall we visit some of them?

Hail one of the smart-looking carriages on the
corner of Canal and St. Charles-streets, (of course
you have a carpet-bag,) and order a drive to the
Ponchartrain Railroad depôt. It is far downward,
and hidden away in a labyrinth of dingy houses
and lane-like streets, but with as open a prospect
when reached as you would desire on a windy day.
It is at the head of the *Champs Elysees*—an avenue like its original only in name, but which,
when the present race of Creoles dies off, *may* be
made one of the healthiest lungs of the Crescent
City. The depôt is a long building, whose founda-
tion as laid by sanguine men of enlarged ideas, is
consecrated to emptiness, and dreary enough in
appearance and feeling for the horse-shed of a
New England " meeting-house." Out of it run
two parallel lines, constructed of strips of iron,
which rest upon the surface of the ground for four
miles, and then cease—these strips of iron are dignified by the name of " Ponchartrain Railroad."
It is so hidden away by sand and grass, and so
swallowed up in a swamp thicket, that it has thus
far escaped the vigilant observation of Doggett,
(Manhattan's favorite Directory son,) who now and

then, with a humane consideration for travelling comfort, issues a Railroad Gazette.

The Ponchartrain Railroad should have a prominent place in the statistical tables of the next census. It is a primitive remnant of railway navigation. It is a relic from the infantile days of the art of steam propulsion, and would be a capital thing to transplant and extend in one of the thousand acre parks of England's fallen railway king, where it would be at once a curiosity and a warning. Aye, transplanted! even with its miniature locomotive, (of one thousand mosquito power,) its sleepy engineer, and ill-contrived, hard-backed, harder-seated cars.

Railroad companies, now-a-days, occasionally declare dividends out of the capital, and therefore are savagely attacked. That were little when one is told that the directors of this four mile railroad declared an immense dividend—*borrowing the money for the purpose!* But some of these days the Gauls who watch over its drowsy finances will have a little Saxon " direction" blood infused into their veins of management, and the railroad will thereafter cease to be the object of tavelling malice.

Over this road you are " ricketed" to the Lake; and if you have ever ridden Turkish fashion over the granite soil of New Hampshire in a farm wagon, you can understand, and only in this event, the meaning of the word " ricketed."

At the end of a long pier running out from a collection of fishing cottages is moored a fine steamer, bound Mobileward. Stepping on board you are soon upon the waters of Lake Ponchartrain, into which, in ages since, emptied the Mississippi, that now rolls sullenly a strip-of-land's breadth off, to give a site to New Orleans.

Squeezing between two forts which guard the rear entrance to the city, (they are separated by a bit of water that New England ideas would call a creek,) Lake Borgne is entered. The "Bay of St. Louis" is the first landing-place; a cozy looking country spot, but owes too much to French domination and French society, and so you pass it by to step ashore at "Pass Christian," the distance of a cannon shot beyond.

Step ashore here, I say, because a gentlemanly host, a well appointed ménage, and an unquarrelled-with-cuisine are great offsets to the monotonous landscape, the teasing mosquitoes, and the ankle-deep sand soil which are to be met with everywhere in the immediate vicinity of New Orleans. The landing is made at a long pier, over which you walk to "Montgomery's Hotel," following a donkey-cart well laden with luggage; planting your feet firmly on the slippery planks, if the wind be fresh, and clambering a steep hill of sand, (by the aid of the glimmering from the light-house tower hard by,) to find at the summit your flagging spirits cheered by the sight of a pleasant smelling garden.

It is not without feelings of apprehension that nervous youths and fidgety old bachelors behold this aforesaid pier of a Saturday night, as the boat they are passengers of approaches the "Pass." Such a collection of white and colored bonnets! Such a waving of delicately-perfumed cambric! Such a bewildering and intoxicating murmur of gentle voices! The men about are in a hopeless minority. The veteran fisherman who all day long sunned himself on the bulkhead, angling, has slipped away long since with timorous steps. The boatmen about but half emerge from places of concealment. It looks very much like a vigorous defence to an invading enemy until the steamers's lines are thrown, and then what a scattering! Poor exiles that these fair ones have been! Husbands, brothers, and lovers for the past week have been in the tiresome, heated city, and Saturday night at Pass Christian (as in the sailor's legend and the olden farce) is a blessed night for sweethearts and wives.

The hotel buildings are drawn up for your approach in true military style—forming a hollow square, with a reserve of apartments attached that stretch out in solid lines—and look out with formidable aspect over the waters of Lake Borgne towards Ship Island, which, in the hazy distance, impertinently obstructs a gulf view for levelled telescopes, and keeps off any matter of surf that seaward gales might beget. The buildings are formed of a numerous collection of doors, windows, and piazzas, more commodious than comfortable; and cooler in interior than is desirable, when the "melancholy days" of rain and gale,

"—— as still such days will come."

succeeded by an Æolian freak—a day of blistering sunlight.

At "Montgomery's," from early June until late October, there is eating and drinking; bowling and flirting; billiards and snoozing; gossip and toilette; driving and novel reading; sailing and yawning; bathing and mosquito scratching; dancing and music. And then the winter long, (a very dreary season on the lake shore, as the rheumatic postmistress confidentially informed me, although a nautical friend who had builded a house on the water-side out of a worn out steamboat, declared his residence was pleasanter in winter than summer,) the wind, mourning the absence of beauty and fashion, will howl about the quadrangles, whistle through the doors and windows, and hum along the quarter-mile piazzas, before it passes on to quarrel with distant rigging, or with the adjacent live-oaks and cypresses, which fill the Mississippian swamp, that from the hotel-back stretches out into a deeper and deeper wilderness of mud and thicket growth.

Further on is Pascagoula and Pensacola—the latter the quietest of all the watering places on the

southern shore; and the former much resorted to
by planters from Alabama and Mississippi, with
their sumptuous equipages, dozens of servants, and
heart-breaking daughter heiresses. Pascagoula has
been called the Newport of the South. In *ton* it
may be; but *ton* has little weight with men, after
tasting Montgomery's pompano, lake trout, and
redfish chowder; and so, I somehow never journeyed past the Pass Christian landing. Besides,
ideas of fashion and exclusiveness vary. As far
as I could see, Montgomery's exactions of body-
coat, and dinner-dresses, were quite rigid enough;
and the intelligent faces, and well stuffed *portes
monnaies* about, had sufficient of the aristocratic
stamp for a quiet man.

I was one night crowded from my accustomed
room into one of the reserve rear buildings, (called
by some waggish fair one "Texas," because they were
refuge places for suspicious nobodies, who quitted
the cities to escape yellow fever, and for play-loving
bachelors, whose midnight card-playing was annoying to delicate nerves, and for disconsolate husbands, whose wives had female friends to turn them
out,) and I wanted, for a chum, either Buckstone, the
farce writer, or Brougham, his transatlantic dramatic prototype. The partition walls of my chamber were thin; in fact the whole building was a
whispering gallery.

Two city clerks, who had left cotton and sugar
for a short period of rustication, were my neigh-

bors. They were full of personal history, frank
and communicative; and although I dropped boot-
jacks, rattled chairs, and scraped my throat with
coughing, not a whit did they seem to heed the
danger of being overheard. One had mingled the
most in society, whereby he had picked up a tolerable smattering of etiquette—about enough to
make him nervous and awkward. His great horror was lest his companion—to use his phrase—
should "*betray their plebian origin*."

"Remember, my boy, we are amidst fashion-
ables. To-day you took soup twice—you skipped
a course"—

"Confound it, Tom, I didn't want that horrid
kidney, which"—

"Never mind; there was plenty else—but listen
—you pared your nails on the piazza, and near by
stood Miss ——, the heiress."

"Good heavens, Tom!"

"Oh horrible! but I have a plan for the future.
Lest any more of these things should "betray our
plebian origin," whenever I see you at table offend-
ing, I'll tread upon your foot."

"Agreed—with one condition—tread on the left
foot, for upon my right is a corn as large as an
apple."

The next morning, at breakfast, I sat near them.
Their toilette was unexceptionable; but the nervous look of the one presented a ludicrous contrast
to the look of effrontery cast up and down the ta-

ble by the other. The betrayer of plebian origin
was about eating an egg, and committing the hei-
nous crime of emptying the shell into a glass, preparatory to the churning process with butter, pep-
per, and salt!

The proceeding caught the eye of the watchful
guardian of etiquette, and down came his foot. I
saw it was on the "corn," by the half-stifled groan
from the injured man, and by the convulsive shutting of the hand, which broke the egg-shell, and
trickled the yolk into his sleeve.

The pain was superior to prudence and self-pos-
session, and the betrayer of plebian origin roared
out, "Tom, it's the wrong foot! confound our plebian origin and your thick boots!"

The astonishment depicted upon the various
faces about, was truly ludicrous. Our heroes beat
a speedy retreat, and at dinner time were marked
upon the register as departed guests.

The Manhattaner who passes a summer at New
Orleans, cannot soon forget "Montgomery's," at
the Pass Christian Watering Place. And of an
August night, with perspiration wreathing my temples, in the breeze deserted city, I sip my claret
to its prosperity, and almost wish myself seated at
the piazza-end, listening to the ripple of the waters,
a stone's throw off, and drinking in, with grateful
lungs, the Caribbean-born breeze, which so noise-
lessly, but effectively, stirs the atmosphere about.

XVI.

Captain Ric's Epithalamium a la Charivari.

"EPITHALAMIUM. A nuptial song, or poem, in praise of the bride and bridegroom, and praying for their prosperity."

So speaks Dr. Noah Webster, from the first half of the gigantic folio, which a minute since fell upon my left foot, and gave a gooseberry twist to my lips. (No small weight, to have half the English language upon your corns!)

And were I sentimentally inclined, (the reader will readily believe the contrary, under the fall of the dictionary,) the solid matter-of-fact definition above quoted, would afford an excellent theme.

There seldom occurs a wedding, unless one of the parties possesses a poetical friend, who exercises his inkstand in composing an epithalamium, (give a broad sound to the second "a," or we shall never get on,) as his quid pro quo, for a slice of

woolly heads, as if timing some invisible music.
The river rolled majestically by, with here and
there on its current the common Mississippi-sight
of a steam tug hugging along some ships, as an ambitious youngster, in display of his strength, might
carry about a couple of teen-ish sisters. I turned
into the avenue, after beckoning a garçon to the
gate, just as my friend with a broad-brimmed straw
hat, (for the sun was winking as if he intended to
be very fiery in intercourse with his darling col-
lateral relation, the earth,) was mounting his little
pony.

"Whither bound, mon ami?"

"Ah, is it you? And so early? To the sugar-
house, on a visit of supervision. Join me, and
we'll back to breakfast in half an hour."

Ten minutes' riding brought us to the sugar-house;
a brick and mortar edifice, suggestive of a New
England factory, with its tall, smoky chimney, and
mill-rolling buzzing.

The encyclopædia at your elbow will spare me
the trouble, reader, and you the weariness of going
through the details of sugar-making; of describing
the long rack, with flexible vertebræ, (inquisition-
reminding machine,) upon which were stretched,
in even layers, the leaf-denuded stalks of cane, to
be whirled up and crushed by rollers, and carried
off, bruised and bleeding; of describing the gutters
and pipes, through which the expressed juice of
the cane ran into kettles, and boilers, and vats,

7

where it was boiled, simmered, stirred, and paddled about by fat negroes, whose shining and sound teeth gave the lie direct to your dentist's idea that sugar injures the enamel, or eats into the cores of your various respectable masticators; or of alluding to the hogsheads, which, filled with wet sugar, stood upon wooden bars, through whose interstices, into vats below, dripped molasses, that in months to come would gladden many a Yankee throat on buckwheat-pancake-day.

"We finish our sugar grinding next week," quoth my friend, "and then we have a bit of merrymaking—a 'king's' ball, at which you must make one of the guests; and a queenly affair it will be."

"A king's ball?"

"Ah, you have not heard. Certain of the youngsters among us, at every yearly winter's ball of the neighborhood, are presented with bouquets by the ladies, who have been the chosen queens of the festivities then concluding; and each bouquet presentee is crowned the king of the next year's ball; being one of the fortunate individuals whose time, purse, and gallantry, are thus placed at the disposal of beauty and fashion. Each king accordingly selects a queen, and under their united auspices the ball is given. So at our forthcoming one you must join our festivities."

And I did.

The parlors of Monsieur De ——'s plantation

mansion were comfortably filled with the Creole beauty and fashion of the parishes of St. Bernard and Plaquemine ; planter's families ; with a small addition of city friends.

[Mem. : Although the general society of New Orleans is still in a chaotic state, and she has no located, acknowledged empire of Japonicadom, and no " upper ten" as yet entered in the relentless ledgers of fashion ; and although generally he who speaks of " moving in the first circles," talks in riddles among the Creoles of country and city " exclusiveness" is a known word, and its meaning properly recognisable by the ten year interlopers of the Second Municipality.]

The complexion of the rooms was decidedly French, and yet with a dash of American feature and manner just sufficient to suggest a contrast.

Creole beauty is not usually of that caste with which to cultivate love at first sight. One must push his acquaintance with it in order to get into raptures and bubble over his fountains of enthusiasm. You see the full black eye ; the raven lustre and classic weight of hair ; and the well-chiselled nose and gracefully met lips. But in their hours of repose their beauty is not striking. In its hour of exhilaration and excitement, however, the Creole beauty of Louisiana will satisfy the most fastidious critic in the æsthetics of physiognomy.

Before me at the ball it was in its triumphant

mood. Then so exquisitely set-off by the thousand minute charms of dress and motion which your true French woman, or French descended woman, can so well adapt to herself.

There were many present of the *ancien regime* of Louisiana. Exclusive; but not cold nor haughty. Proud they are; yet affable. Exacting of etiquette to a hair line; yet hospitable; and none more so. I was soon (although among strangers) as much at home in feeling as if my memory had learned and moulded their growing features day after day, from early childhood.

The ringing laugh; the merry music; and the shadows of the dancers and masquers at that "coast ball," will be among my most pleasurable reminiscences of the South.

As I stood by an open window refreshing myself after a quadrille, with the puffs of river air coming gratefully inward, and there looking admiringly and musingly upon the gay scene before me, my friend touched my shoulder and called my attention to the glorious couple who were whirling in one of Julien's waltzes, while the eyes of the idlers became intently fixed upon them.

"Are they not worthy of the admiration their appearance elicits?"

I nodded assent.

"Man and wife—in the prime of life, with forty years figured down for them in the old bible at their Knickerbocker. early home; yet as buoyant in feeling and tender in intercourse as though they were lovers."

"Lovers! there's a story in your eye—I see it. Take a seat in this recess, and narrate without any allusions to 'long ago' or 'once upon a time,' if you please."

"They *were* lovers, and thereby hangs the tale. She was an idolized belle, when he was a bashful sophomore at college with his books. She was a finished woman while he was yet an awkward boy. They met at his mother's house; and as he gazed into her liquid eyes, and listened to her joyous voice, hopes and thoughts, new and exhilarating, were born in his soul. Their opportunities of society became frequent. While he made her his idol, and loved as youth only loves, without reason or analysis, she looked upon him as a younger brother—laughed at his jokes—teased his whilom nervousness—praised his rhymes, (of which she was the inspiring muse,) and accepted his escort to soirée and concert when beaux more promising but less faithful failed in their punctual homage. Years passed on. Many were her offers of marriage; her refusals were frequent. He grew more manly; loving as blindly, as devotedly as ever; and as secretly—for as yet no thought of his idolatry crossed her mind, or was impelled into utterance by his speech or action. The slight difference of age, his instinct taught him, was fatal to his hopes. Avowal might bring rebuke, and rebuke banishment. He reflected as the months rolled on, and reflection summoned to his relief prudence. He accepted voluntary banishment, and left New York—for that was their residence—for New Orleans, which was in the infancy of its prosperity, and the *ultima Thule* of domestic emigration.

"The parting was agonizing to him; for a thousand hopes died in that hour; and the calmness of his adieu was frightful to her vision. For the first time she suspected his love. He reached New Orleans; and in the study of Louisiana law, intricate in practice and abstruse in detail, forgot for a time the power and majesty of his love. Ambition succeeded beauty as his idol. Hours there were when the memory of his early love, returned in power as of old; but in study and mental toil and ambitious aspiration, that power was lessened of its sting.

"She made a *marriage de convenance* with a money-broker to oblige her father; and in the frigidity of her husband's soul was as unhappy as one of her generous impulses and affectionate dispositions always must be when meeting with no return of sympathy. Her husband failed. So did her father. Both died; and she and her family were destitute.

"Her early lover had remained single, had amassed wealth, and was earning the proud distinction of a name. News of her position reached him, and in the midst of winter, with the pressure of a large business on his shoulders, he left New Orleans, and journeyed to New York. They met. Time had but set the seal of all glorious matured loveliness upon her brow.*

"And in the usual style of the Ladies' books—I've read such tales a hundred times—they were married and he relieved everybody from difficulty."

"You guess at the exact sequel. But my story has one merit, and it is as true as the compass points in the quadrangle through yonder window. They *were* married. She returned with him to the sunny south, and the years of both of them freshened by the memories of youth, and the realization on his part of hopes long thought dead, and on her part of a happiness doubly grateful by its contrast with the past. It is ten years since this. And they are as trusting and confiding as ever. Inseparable even in society, and bold against the etiquette of Creole customs, as you saw by their whirling together in yonder waltz. He was king of the ball, and chose her as queen. Both things innovations. But their story is known and appreciated; and they are courted everywhere, and all they do admired."

---

* " The last
The ripest seal of loveliness was set
Upon her form."——

LORD IVON BY WILLIS.

XV.

LEVEES AND CREVASSES. THE FATHER OF WA-
TERS IN CORRESPONDENCE WITH THE PENOB-
SCOT RIVER.

"TAKING in contemplation New Orleans as a
whole, what dy'e think of it?" asked an
"old settler" of an acquaintance-stranger, in my
hearing.

"As a hole? you're depreciative and——"

"No—no—none of your waggeries; I mean
balancing the advantages and the disadvantages of
locality, climate, et cetera."

"Well then to be candid," continued he who
was buttonholed, and whose uncle had been in
correspondence with Preissnetz " *I think it is a par-
adise for a water-cure hospital !*"

I am certain there are few nervous ladies and
gentlemen, who, if they *could* be induced to make

a short ascent in a balloon from any portion of
New Orleans, and so take a bird's-eye view of its
situation would consent to inhabit its precincts
without the preparation of a life-boat in their gar-
rets, or at least the latest improvement of a life-
preserver in their pockets. They would see the
liquid wall which surrounds the city, and which,
if toppled over some day, might call forth from
any epistolary "Toots" to a correspondent at the
north the expression of the great original to 'Lieu-
tenant' Walters when the latter narrated his escape
from shipwreck—"I'm afraid you must have got
very wet." However, the Orleanois treat the idea
of incursion from "old Mississippi" as a humorous
absurdity. Their scepticism of security has been
sorely tried, however, in two or three recent in-
stances of crevasses which have induced the con-
struction of a transverse levee from river to lake
(very much to the horror of the back-settlers who
have their own private opinion of the selfishness
predominant in large cities.) The "Father of
Waters" as it sweeps its mischievous eddies around
the circling banks eyes the crops to the right and
left with a very spiteful glance. I have seen a
million dollars worth of property—plantations;
field lands; sugar-houses, and their ponderous machinery; family mansions, and live stock, at the
mercy of a narrow mound of clay and sod that a
vigorous ditch-digger on a New England farm
often equals in strength by the accumulation of
7*

random spadings of soil. It has so often been in the power of an indolent and reckless planter (owner, perhaps, of a few hundred acres, and who sends some twenty hogsheads of sugar to his factor with instructions to "hold on" for a stubborn price in hopes of a "lull" in the market) to suffer a devastation of his neighbor's property to enrich his own with a deposit of soil from the vagrant river, that the miracle is, not that one hears of so few crevasses on the Mississippi, but that there are not perpetual ones. I know I will be referred to statute-books, (Verbo: "Levees,") and expected to read pages of directions and penalties; or told of the gangs of field hands and Levee Inspectors required to be at work in certain seasons on weak points; but, nevertheless, Mississippi is a sly rascal, and will often, with the aid of a small crawfish, which a starving Irishman would barely deign to eat, undermine in a few nights the month's labors of a dozen gangs of "Mound Builders."

"Enrich his own land with a deposit of soil!" repeats some reader dashing the sentence with a "quere." That the Mississippi water is heavy with mud any juvenile geographer knows; but the quantity of "settlings" left behind in one season on submerged land will be scarcely credited save by eye-witnesses. I was shown some six hundred acres of land on a plantation below New Orleans that some ten or twelve years ago was "manufactured" on worthless swamp land by a season's irrigation. The law of accretion which in the Code

Napoleon is rather a fancy subject, becomes eminently practical to the thumbers of the civil code of Louisiana. There are now pending suits under the law which, in their discussion, have shaken to the verge of concussion the brains of dead and worm-eaten New Orleans lawyers, and which, to all appearance, bid fair to afford years of handsome livings to civilians yet unborn.

The Crevasse! ominous words these two, to dwellers in the lower Mississippi; as ominous as puzzling to the northern uninitiated. Out with your Webster, Walker or Richardson, (according to the dictionary you swear by,) and pencil for the word this definition; "Crevasse. A word expressing a break made by the force of a river-current in a levee or dyke. N. B. The word is very common in New Orleans papers, and in the dry season a great bugbear to northern editors.

There have been very serious ones occurring on the Mississippi River, since I had the pleasure of airing my carpet-bag in New Orleans; but I had opportunity of settling my breakfast with the sight of a small one, by the aid of Philanthropist McDonough's* ferry-boat. The river had been insulted, no doubt, by the number of launches that the busy town of Algiers (opposite New Orleans) yearly inflicted upon him, and so one fine morning, before sluggish mortals were wide awake, he made a sudden sweep upon the various ship-yards of its vi-

---

* See appendix.

cinity, and sported famously upon a race-course
hard by. Crevasse! Crevasse! was echoed by by-
standers early on 'change; and re-echoed by many,
as they would cry out, Mad bull! to an elderly
lady wearing a red shawl, in the vicinity of a china-
ware shop. I took a preliminary observation from
the dome of the St. Charles, (where one will always
be safe from watery accidents, unless they come
cloud-wise,) and satisfied myself that the town of
Algiers, unless something was done for it in the engineering way, would become a species of Hercu-
laneum for diving-bell amateurs of the day; although the waggish book-keeper of the establishment insisted that the "Father of Waters" was
complimenting Algiers by giving it a *bay*. In
other words, it was all *day* with it. When I crossed
over in the ferry-boat, I found sundry municipal
and parish functionaries laying their heads together,
in endeavors to stop the rush of many waters coming through a break some hundred feet wide, at
the rate of six or seven miles an hour. Not that
they thrust their heads into the breach, as the
"Little Hero of Dutch Harlem," immortalized in
Sharpe's Magazine, thrust his finger into the leak
in the village dyke! The more the authorities
consulted, the swifter ran the current; sundry
houses were up to their eyes in water; there was
no time for resolutions of enquiry, and appoint-
ments of committees with power to act; so they
threw the responsibility upon an engineer, who, in

a day or two of sturdy fighting with timber piles, straw, sand-bags, and dismembered steamboat hulks, wrote himself down, in the annals of Algiers, as its saviour. But there was a deal of dredging, and sweeping, and spading done within its precincts, for many a day afterward; and the track of the Bingaman Race-course, that had been made the passing medium of communication with rear swamps, remained, for a long period, as "heavy" as the heaviest better on the best bottomed horse, on a stormy rainy day, could have desired.

The crevasses happening since then, have made the one I speak of to be remembered as a mere incident. I did not see them; but I have a good idea of the current tearing over thousands of well ordered plantations; "sucking in" (as the phrase goes) heavy steamboats, with sleepy pilots; and freshening the Gulf of Mexico at new points. Their occurrence, and the remedies applied, no doubt suggested the following bit of correspondence, picked up in a recent eastern freshet, and delicately penned on the top of a sugar hogshead stave:—

THE MISSISSIPPI TO THE PENOBSCOT.

My Dear Penobscot:

That you have lately had no communication with your father—the Father of Waters—has not been my fault; and now you are not indebted to my paternal solicitude only for these brief messages, but also to the eccentricities of a chemist, who dipped up the caskfull containing these reflections, to mix with your own bright and crystal bubblings.

I have read in some newspapers hid away in my bosom, and stolen from the cabin of a snagged steamboat, that the wretched men of your neighborhood are about damming you upon a large scale, and curbing your mettle, at various points, into an unpleasant stagnation; to stun you with the noise and whirl of machinery; to blacken your hopes with filthy dyes; and stain your virgin purity with mountains of clay and charred timber. I can advise you, in such a crisis; for I, too, have been hardly dealt with, and have only lately learned how to punish our oppressor, man, for his various audacities and contumelies. As you well learned, before civilization, with its barriers of confused noise, intercepted our conversations, I was once freer than now. I could stretch myself, when wearied, over miles and miles of land; I could venture on a pic-nic far into the primeval forests of the country; I could play pranks with the war-parties, and tribe-hunts of the early Indians; I could surprise the deer at his drinking, and overpower him where the arrows of pursuers were hurtless; if the great gulf, to whose luxury I administer, at any time ruffled my temper, my liquid products sought outlet into the many bays about him. But the conqueror came, and fenced me in, and dug into my very vitals, and gave me heavy burdens to bear, and hideous noises to listen to, and bade my roaring propensities cease, while my course of life was made as monotonous as that of our bastard relatives, the canals. For how many years have I fretted and fumed at all these outrages! I have leagued with your remote brother, the Missouri, (a wild, untamed fellow,) the Ohio, (a gentle and lovely daughter,) the Red River, (a perfect savage,) the Yellow Stone, (a spiritless vagabond,) and with increased strength made repeated efforts to regain my former liberty. Perhaps, in your quiet nook, you may have heard of the fright I last year gave to my largest city; and how bravely I fought it, week after week, until compelled, by sheer exhaustion, to give in. (I ruined the reputation of two surveyors—that's some consolation.) But this year, the victory is mine. I have avoided the city; it contains material too powerful. I have directed my forces against interior places. I could contain myself no longer. Was I not choking with the secretions of old age? Was I not becoming asthmatic, through compression of my lungs? Were not my oppressors threatening to dredge out the Falls of St. Anthony, and hammer and forge me far towards my very source? I made my selections; and this early spring-time made a dash at Vicksburg, and at the parishes lower down. Houses, and sugar-factories, cotton and cane, have all been swept before me. I am as free as ever. I have expanded myself twenty miles at one point. I have made a dozen new channels for future use at other points. I have united myself, as of old, to Lake Ponchartrain, and thrilling, even in my old age, are her kisses. I may again be vanquished and imprisoned. But oh, my oppressor man, leave me my fond lake to meet day after day, and I will withdraw forever from the contest!

You, my Penobscot, are young and lusty. Keep cool for a time. Let the timbers fall across you, and the stones and sand choke you. Bide your revenge. The winter is coming. Freeze hard; freeze low; melt quickly; summon all your energies; quicken the flow of your arteries; come out in swelling grandeur; and all the timbers and masonry of the land may not resist you.

I would say more; but the cask of the chemist is full, and my words would be wasted. Imagine the waving of adieu from your almost heartbroken father,

MISSISSIPPI.

XVI.

Captain Ric's Epithalamium à la Charivari.

" EPITHALAMIUM. A nuptial song, or poem, in praise of the bride and bridegroom, and praying for their prosperity."

So speaks Dr. Noah Webster, from the first half of the gigantic folio, which a minute since fell upon my left foot, and gave a gooseberry twist to my lips. (No small weight, to have half the English language upon your corns!)

And were I sentimentally inclined, (the reader will readily believe the contrary, under the fall of the dictionary,) the solid matter-of-fact definition above quoted, would afford an excellent theme.

There seldom occurs a wedding, unless one of the parties possesses a poetical friend, who exercises his inkstand in composing an epithalamium, (give a broad sound to the second "a," or we shall never get on,) as his quid pro quo, for a slice of

cake and a bridal kiss.   The number of these bridal poems now lying in the portfolios of the world,
fragrant with sighs, and, perhaps, with tears, must
be impossible of computation; although Hymen's
torch comes in contact with the rhythm so often, it
is no small wonder they are not burned into ashes.

Now I have often remarked, in the course of
these papers, that New Orleans was a very matter-
of-fact place, and induced small poesy of feeling.
(How the "Gazettes" collect so much of the latter,
week by week, is a puzzle to me.)

Be visibly surprised, then, to know that the definition of our long heading-word is by no means
unknown in New Orleans; and that the composers
of epithalamiums, upon many occasions, are numbered by the score; quite putting to the blush, in
their assemblage, the classical collections of ancient
humanity, termed choruses, whose doings and sayings may be thoroughly comprehended, on application to any college freshman.

Long before the word democracy assumed the
power of a thunderbolt, it indulged its freedom of
speech and opinion in France, and in England, upon
the suitability of matrimonial matches.   Not in the
gentlemanly way of fireside scandal, and tea-table
gossip, but by demonstrations forcible and convincing.   The old man and maiden, or the widow
of maturity and the beardless youth, coupling
themselves together before God and man, were met

with the frowns and arrows of outraged public propriety.

To tell *how*, must be left to the chroniclers. I say thus much only by way of preface to the fact, that democracy of sentiment in New Orleans sits in similar judgment at the present day.

The epithalamiums of the "Sheet Iron Band" are proper municipal records in the Crescent City. The Mayor and the Recorders do not sign them; nor do clerks of courts copy them; but patriarchal authority, nevertheless, by winks and nods, affixes its sign-manual to their binding character. And he has passed a winter in New Orleans to little purpose, who has never heard of the Sheet Iron Band, or made acquaintance with its gallant captain, whose head, by this time, must be as full of epithalamiums, as are his notarial records of marriage contracts.

Who the Sheet Iron Band may be, as a *public body*, is a matter of question. Individually, they are "fellow-citizens," and musical doctors; they are perpetual advertisers and puffers of acoustic oil; they are strong and lusty; they are fond of horns; they are men of brass; they are given to irony; they appear "in the dim and dusky twilight," like the Israelites around Jericho, or the beleaguering army about the walls of Prague, upon the simple summons of their captain through the daily prints.

Their captain, however, is a notable. He is a Czar of music; an Autocrat of noise; and carries

in his hand the wand of Prospero, with which, by
hook or crook, in some way unknown, he summons his Ariels to greet, with noise of horns and
trumpets, tin pans and sheet iron, the unequally‧
yoked brides and bridegrooms; making the latter
to cry out like Ferdinand to *his* Ariel:—

> "Hell is empty,
> And all the devils are here."

Disparity of age in matrimony is the crime to
be punished; to be punished by fine, the proceeds
whereof go to the support of charity. Neither
rest at night, nor quiet of mind by day, knows the
victim bridegroom, until the fine is paid.

The sanguine youth who is on his knees to a
venerable spinster, and her money-bags, associates
his thoughts of betrothal with fears of the Sheet
Iron Band. The gouty millionaire, who totters to
the feet of mammon-infatuated girlhood, sees
through the blushes of his future wife the smiles
of "Captain Ric," as he sits at his table to draw up
his company orders. Of little use is obstinacy,
pluck, and nerves of steel; the captain and his
men are superior. In the contest of mouth against
ears, muscles against nerves, perseverance against
resolution, experience, after weeks of siege, has
proved Captain Ric invincible.

I observed him a summer ago in the hall of the
Astor House. It was after dinner, and I saw by
the sparkle of his eye that the flavor of the Hock

was yet lingering about his palate. He sat on the railing, cracking jokes for a half dozen friends, and as many waiters, who were stealthily at hand. His glossy hat was on one side. His vest was flashy as the gown of a dowager. His chains were suggestive of California. The turned-down collar, and figured cravat, bespoke him the southerner. The reaped stubble on his face was like the ashes of roses. His shiny boots insulted the atmosphere with their swinging. His cane was at rest on his knees, and his voice rang through the hotel lobbies as I was used to hear it in the Commercial Exchange, on St. Charles-street, when he was beating up recruits for the Mexican war, in a dress of "Attakapas mixed," with a bright red sash about his waist.

I thought then of the time I last observed him; on the outskirts of the Swamp Faubourg of New Orleans, of a foggy November night, seated on the bank of a ditch, surrounded by his Sheet Iron Band, endeavoring to blow out of a miserly Dutchman, who had married his young housekeeper, a few dollars for the Sisters of Charity. It was in Hercules-street, and the attempt, in other hands, would have been Herculean indeed.

There once lived in New Orleans a fair spinster, whose mother had been a West Indian Creole, and a schoolmate of the Empress Josephine. She was proud and rich, relationless and single, and no one seemed to share her confidence or sympathy except a lanky, gray haired notary, whose den was in Lower Royal-street. He bought and sold her slaves, leased her houses, collected her dividends, and paraded her large tin cash box in a conspicuous place within his office, as if to say, "trust in me, for I am notary and agent to Mademoiselle——"

One evening our notary was sitting in his chair, in a musing attitude, watching a mouse nibbling a hole in a map. It was raining out-doors, and the street was silent and almost deserted. Nevertheless he felt cheerful, for his attorney had that day "put through" the Court of Probates, on a succession tableau, the sum of five hundred dollars for "services" rendered the estate. And it was a sure thing, too. The heir in France, when the per centage to the State was deducted, and the costs all paid, might receive half that sum, and might grumble; but no matter, the fish were caught in his net, and he'd fry them. Perhaps he was thinking of the heir; for, when the door suddenly opened, he jumped from his chair and seized his ruler.

"*Bon soir, Monsieur,*" said a voice—the voice of his aforesaid client, coming out of a pile of cloaks, which were being taken off by a brace of mulattresses, who performed escort duty with umbrellas.

"*Bon soir, Mademoiselle,*" stammered the notary, although not forgetting the appropriate emphasis on the latter word, so ear-tickling to the ears of fifty; and handing a chair.

The lady sat down and began blowing off the excitement of her pedestrian war with the elements; and our notary had leisure for surmise.

"What *was* in the wind? Was she seized with premonitions of dissolution, and had she come to make her will? Had she discovered that last surplusage of per centage? Never before had she been known to dare the rains of December, or the muddy trottoirs of Royal-street."

"I have come," at last breathed the lady, (she always breathed her words, instead of speaking them, and I would her breathing could be translated like her French,) to employ you to draw a marriage contract."

The notary bowed, and asked himself what relation had turned up at last.

"Between Mademoiselle ——."

"Why, that's yourself," shrieked the notary, squeezing his pen to atoms of splits.

"Most certainly; but don't call so loud; the neighbors will hear; between myself, then, and Monsieur ——."

"Why, that's my clerk!" re-shrieked the notary, tossing the pen furiously from him.

"Undoubtedly," replied the imperturbable breather, while the servants by the door nudged umbrellas.

"Ask me to draw up a marriage contract between yourself and my clerk, whom I picked up on the levee, just out of a Havre emigrant ship?

It is an insult. Oh, if you want to marry, marry me!" continued the notary, with his eye on the cash-box, (for well he knew, whoever the groom might be, the real bride was under its green lid.)

"A very nice gentleman—so polite—so well dressed—the son of an exiled Count—and we arranged it last night—he is young and you are old —for your past services I forgive you your allusions, but henceforth discharge you"—were breathed out gradually. And the breathing, and the cloaks, and umbrellas, prepared to go.

As the door closed upon them the notary laughed —he was himself—remembrances of that fee returned, and he muttered the words, "Sheet-Iron-Band."

The old lady and her escort turned up town. "I'll have it drawn to-night or never," said she. "To-night or never," whistled the wind as it swept by her cloaks and tore over the umbrella.

The office of one notary is passed—and another —and of a third; but they were closed. The Post-Office building is reached. She looked opposite in hopes of a light, but there was none; and Gottschalk's drug lights blending with those flashing from the Exchange-bar made the only illumination visible.

The high stoop of the building adjoining, in which the most gentlemanly of all created notaries was wont to bow receipts for fees, and smile acknowledgments through his juvenile spectacles,

was too great a climb. Still onward to the Musson
buildings under the British Consulate. (Oh, that
she were English and could rush for a marriage
contract under the recent act of Victoria to the office where so much bonhommie is im-mure-d from
November to July!)

She was now in Canal-street—about to cross it.
Never had she been there before; she was passing
the Rubicon of Creole prejudice, and entering on
the American portion of the city.

Still onward to the Verandah hotel: where, as
if frightened by the shadows of the gigantic St.
Charles, she turned the corner.

But soon halted, as a bright light came flashing
through her cloaks, and bringing with it almost
the only English word she knew, "Notary," from
a large sign hard by.

Crossing the street, or rather fording it, she
looked inside the building.

Sure enough, it *was* a Notary's office. There
were the big folios; the tin boxes; the maps; and
the hard seats. Upon one of them sat "Captain
Ric;" and *he* was the owner of the office!

Captain Ric spoke French in his way, and soon
learned enough for the purpose; the contract was
drawn, and the hour the next day appointed for its
signing. When the clerkly groom was there, and
Captain Ric and a brace of authentic witnesses;
and the carriages ordered for the cathedral were
standing by the door; and the umbrella-carriers of

the night before were teeth-grinning over the salvers that held the cake and wine.

Holy Church said its blessing on the bride, who breathed her responses in a feeling manner; and upon the bridegroom, who, while the priest was mumbling his Latin, entered into a nice calculation of what the usufruct of his settlement was worth, and wondered where was located his property which the facetious Notary had duly impressed on his mind was thenceforth subject to a tacit mortgage.

The happy couple were not subscribers to the "Picayune" or they would have seen in its columns, the ensuing day, a modest card of anonymous authority, calling on the Sheet-Iron-Band to appear that night for duty. Why and where was left to be told by Captain Ric, who was about to use his Notarial knowledge for charitable purposes.

Night came on, and Esplanade-street was black with items of humanity. Levee clerks were there with horns and tops of grate-pans. Tchoupitoulas-street clerks were there with stove-pipes and pokers. An amateur from Jefferson-parish was there with a Kent bugle, and a pair of lungs which would have been a matter of capital for the forges at the Novelty Works. Trombones and fifes; a modest drum; and a cat-call exiled from the Bowery Theatre pit were sprinkled through the crowd; and all arranged before the house of the *happy* pair.

What noises came upon the midnight air for two full hours let the habitans about the Mint and even up to Circus-street, narrate—noises which would have driven whole tribes of Indians mad for very envy, could they have heard them. Noises which brought the druggist hard by to his window with dozens of bottles of acoustic oil, freshly làbelled. Noises which composed the nuptial song or poem; but whether in praise of bride or bridegroom I cannot, under favor of Dr. Webster's goodly definition, say. Perhaps of the bride, for, as was before remarked, she had breathing powers worthy of compliment.

But they accomplished their purpose, and when the purse of " yellow boys" came from an upper window the noises died away. And Captain Ric was seen to lead away a lanky, grey-haired man who had almost blown himself senseless with a fish-horn.

It was the spurned Notary of Royal-street, who had been taking revenge!

XVII.

RIDE TO THE BATTLE-GROUND—A STORY OF
THE EVENTS OF THE BRITISH ATTACK ON
NEW ORLEANS IN 1815.

I HAVE spoken of the Ponchartrain Railroad,
and properly recognised its claims to be consid-
ered a remnant of primitive railroad management.
I ought not to forget mention of its neighbor,
which runs out of the same street, at right angles
to the road first named, and possesses a similar
barn of a depôt, and similar Lilliputian energies,
and train of hard-backed cars—the Mexican Gulf
Railroad—a *chemin de fer* not much better than the
Ponchartrain, but more *promising* in the future;
and extending towards the Gulf of Mexico easterly,
for a greater distance, through a much finer section
of country.

When some opportune earthquake shall come to
the aid of its directors—digging out and inclosing

a proper harbor at its terminus—the original aims of its founders and the hopes of its enthusiastic president will be fulfilled, and the road be used for other than mere excursionary purposes, by listless time-killers and zealous Waltonians, who desire not a breathing upon the transit of their sheep-head and red-fish from native element to the frying-pan or chowder-pot.

Some three or four miles of travel on this Mexican Gulf Railway will bring you to the spot famous in American history as the locality where, in January, 1815, the American forces, under command of General Jackson, obtained a victory over the British invaders of Louisiana, and drove them from its soil with great and disproportionate slaughter. The spot is well known to orators and poetasters as the *Plains of Chalmette.*

One fine day in early spring-time I had the good fortune to visit it, in company with one who had been participant in the deeds of that occasion; one who every year figures in an immense barouche as a "veteran of 1815," at the head of a military street procession, when the citizens of New Orleans, with patriotic punctuality, celebrate the victory of Jackson and his comrades.

"Here we are," said he, as the cars stopped by the side of a very unpoetical ditch, and in view of immense fields of planted sugar cane, about six inches high, a thick swamp wood on our left, and the turbid Mississippi at our right.

"This the battle-ground?" replied I, rubbing my limbs and arms, by way of compound interest upon the dimes invested in the jolting ride.

"Aye, the battle-ground!" he rejoined with eloquent emphasis; thirty-two years of intermediate life rolling away from before his glowing vision, as he thought of the day when, on the spot before him, he battled an invading enemy. "Here is the place where so many brave subjects of King George took their last look on the objects of this life. Brave fellows they were; for I never want to see greater exertions in the very jaws of death than were made that day by the troops of General Pakenham."

"But before your after-reflections, my dear veteran, give me a methodical story of the affair. It will come pat and interesting, with the very ghosts of the illustrious and departed heroes flitting through these rows of sugar cane. And here's a moistener of your memory, in the shape of some *eau de vie*, 1805—ten years before your battle."

Veteran [taking a pull.] "I'm no hand for stories, and have been over the ground so often that—"

Manhattaner. "Over the ground so often;" that's a good pun.

V. No undue interruption,—that I make out but slip-shod rhethoric. *N'importe*, there's a belles-

lettres savor about your cordial. But to begin.
You remember how unfortunately for us the incursion of the British in Maryland turned out;
and how little, nevertheless, of advantage was attained by the invaders. And how that soon afterwards the British fleet, with the soldiers on board,
and sundry reinforcements, appeared in the Gulf,
meditating an attack upon New Orleans.

M. Who can forget these items! And you
might add to the list the coquetting between the
Spanish authorities of Florida and the British
leaders; not to forget the "self-responsibility" of
old Hickory's summary treatment of the Spanish
Governor for his military flirtation.

V. We in New Orleans had very exaggerated
ideas of the invading movement. We were in uncertainty, too, as to where the attack would be
made. Those were not the days of steam-frigates,
and we were not afraid of any entrance over the
bar and passage, against the Mississippi current,
by the ships of war. The British had enough of
taking the latter into interior waters, when invading Chesapeake Bay. So our attention was mostly
directed to guarding the city by the little lakes.
The enemy had studied our topography, and had
their eyes upon the Rigolets, and the Peninsular
strip of land which separated the river and the
gulf. About the 10th of December, the ships an-
chored off Cat and Ship Islands—you have seen

them from your window at "Montgomery's," while summering at the Pass.

M. And explored both of them, on divers fishing excursions, with that prince of accomplished gentlemen, General S—— of Concordia. Pleasant spots both of them for a misanthrope; asylums, mayhap, for decayed statesmen!

V. The Spanish fishermen on the coast had given information that Jackson had some five thousand men only, as available; and but sixteen hundred of these near the city. Whereat the soldiery were much delighted with so encouraging a prospect of invasion. The enemy were cautious, however. They sounded for the best information of a landing-place; and it turned out afterwards Lieut. Peddie of the army, in the disguise of a Spanish fisherman, made a reconnoitre of the coast. He reported that a little bayou or canal, called Bienvenue by the natives, and connecting General Villeré's plantation with the Gulf, was just the place to accomplish a landing. It was but ten or twelve miles below the city, and a short distance from where we are. Of course we had gun-boats and that sort of thing upon the lakes. Very well they were manned, too, and bothered the British considerably. But the navigation of Lake Borgne, and the bays about, was very uncertain. A good strong north-westerly wind exposes flats enough for the gambols of a thousand mermaids, and the low water was the cause of the capture of some of their number, and the withdrawal of the remainder. We had rumors of all these things in the city, where all was activity and quick thought. General Jackson was pretty much emperor of the city, and his sayings were law. It seemed despotic to those at a distance; but it was necessary.

M. I can understand how. Your population was mixed. No concert or harmony of opinion. And in consequence of the changes and shiftings of civil rule in previous years, the sands in the hour-glasses of the municipal authorities did not fall so regularly as they should.

V. And it was well Jackson was the man in command, for some of the legislators then in session, were very nervous and undecided. The citizens were wide awake. The women were making clothing for the volunteers expected from up the river, and known to be in want of seasonable habiliments. Children were running bullets. On the 18th of December, Jackson reviewed the militia— a battalion of colored men among them, who handled the musket very well, considering how much more familiar they were wlth hoes, and hogsheads, and bales.

So things went on, until the 23d, two days before Christmas. In the morning arrived the Tennesseeans, who encamped above the city. About noon in came a son of General Villeré breathless with haste and excitement, with the news that over two thousand of the enemy, with General Keane,

8*

had boated through Canal Bienvenue, and were occupying his family plantation.

M. Twelve miles from the city, you said.   Close quarters that, and a handful, as it were, of raw militia, to combat disciplined regulars.

V. No sooner was this heard than Jackson was on the move.   Carrol's and Claiborne's brigades were left to guard the rear approaches of the city ; for he knew not what diversion the British might make from Lake Ponchartrain.   The little war schooner, Carolina, was ordered to drop down the river, and occupy a position on the opposite bank to the Villeré plantation.   By nightfall of that day the little force under General Coffee was at the enemy, penetrating into their camp while some of them were at supper.

M. Egad, they got hotter *coffee* than they expected.

V. And *Carolina* potatoes of a wrong sort for comfortable digestion.   The little schooner poured a perfect shower of shot into the enemy's camp, and compelled a remove further back from the river.   The British were completely at disadvantage, taken by surprise ; and their loss was severe. Our men—particularly the civilians, *militaire pour le moment,*—were somewhat too impetuous, and in the darkness of the night, some of them were separated from their comrades, and taken prisoners. We lost about seventy-five men in that way.

M. Our legal friend ——, was of the number.

He complained bitterly of the bad feed he got for several days, and of the horridly stupid conversation he was compelled to listen to. To believe his yarns, I'm thinking the midnight attack and the capture of prisoners was a good thing for General Jackson. It gave him a prestige and every prisoner multiplied his force *ad libitum*—mere legal fictions you know!

V. Perhaps so. But by daybreak Jackson had retreated for a short distance; and the morning light showed him what a fine position he was in for an entrenchment. Before him was this fine plain now stretching out before us. The river and the schooners Carolina and Louisiana protected his right flank; the cypress swamp his left flank. There was a canal in front, (it had a name then— Rodriguez,) which could be deepened; and behind it raised a wall of clay and other materials (the latter cotton bags, as you know—they are famous now in American history.) Immediately the necessary means were employed, and in two days a perfectly secure fortification protected New Orleans from the enemy.

M. I have always wondered why the British leaders remained idle so long: why they allowed the making of these entrenchments without attack.

V. It was a great mistake. But they had a poor opinion of our engineering; and regarded our troops as mere handfuls to the antagonist force they expected to bring.   Besides, all their troops were not landed.   At daybreak on the twenty-eighth the enemy were descried advancing in two columns; one on the river road; one by the margin of the swamp.   A brief engagement ensued, in which they were repulsed with great loss to themselves, and but little to our own.   This temporary check satisfied their invading disposition, and they awaited the reinforcements which were expected with General Lambert.   They next set about erecting three batteries—one at the river side, one at the swamp edge, and one directly before our position; with a parapet of clay in line, the embrasures of which were cased with sugar hogsheads. These latter were unfortunate things to use, as it subsequently turned out.   They thought the sugar would afford an elastic resistance to shot like as sand; but the cannon balls drove through it, and many were injured by the splinters from the hogsheads.   This was but three hundred yards distant from us.   A cold and cheerless time they had of it.   It was the rainy season of the year; drizzle and fogs; and water all about them from a breach in the Levee made by the orders of Jackson, through which sullenly flowed the Father of waters to pay his respects to the new-comers.

M. Pooh! drizzle and fogs were the very things they liked.   Why should a British soldier be different from a British sailor who got drunk with delight while entering the fog-bewildered docks of

London one November day after " a month of lay-
ing-to in the miserable sunshine of Naples!"

V. New-Years's eve was a busy time for the
enemy. How they worked with pickaxes and
shovels! They were in good earnest, too, as you
might see by the shoulder-knots of officers bobbing
up and down at their labors.

M. And you a nice distance off watching them
as coolly as a butcher regards a grazing ox whose
fate is sealed for a holiday-dinner. Did you make
no demonstration?

V. How foolish that would have been? They
expected we would have come out to meet them;
but in a field fight we knew where the odds lay.
Five thousand against twelve thousand! No odds
when Mexicans are in the maximum catalogue;
but " when Greek meets Greek," etc. On New-
Year's morning they commenced cannonading us
from their batteries; and we returned the compliment with compound interest, dislodging their
cannon in a few hours, and forcing them to fall
back in a new position.

M. What were the sloops-of-war doing?

V. The poor Carolina was fastened in position
by the current. There was no wind; and after a
brave return of cannon shot to some mounted batteries on the river bank of the British camp, a few
hot shot wrapped her in flames. The Louisiana
was more fortunate, and weighed anchor out of
their gun-reach. The overflowing of the plain

below our position was unfortunate in one respect, as it assisted the British in their exertions to bring up cannon and ammunition from the fleet. For five days in January they worked at the digging a canal from the Gulf to their camp. And thus by the seventh of January the British force, by the arrival of General Lambert's reinforcement numbered twelve thousand. Some of the prisoners of the twenty-third fortunately escaped, and gave us an inkling of what was to be *l'ordre du jour.*

M. Twelve thousand men ! the flower of the British army ! How well they must have appeared from your position !

V. " Ah !" (heaving a sigh with a pull at the cordial flask,) you are thinking of some holiday parade on your New York Park grounds upon some sunny day. Faith, *mon cher ami,* they didn't appear at all by reason of the fog which was heavy enough to give the cows a bronchitis, and as disagreeable to breathe as the smoke of a cabbage-leaf regalia cigar. The signal—so the escaped prisoners told us—was to be the ascent of two rockets at either wing of their army. We watched for the pyrotechnic display with more earnest attention than any juvenile escaped from school employs at London-Vauxhall, or Gotham-Niblo's when the fire-works are momently expected. The Barrataria pirates and some veteran French cannoneers were our artillerists at the embrasures of the entrenchment. Behind them were the sharpest

shooters of the force—Tennesseeans and Keutuck-
ians (who were as cool as if out on a buffalo hunt,)
with their rifles. And relays of men behind to
load, that there might be no intermission in the
firing. Squadrons of cavalry were at the right and
left flank, and in the rear. On the morning of the
eighth the looked-for signal was seen, and hailed
with loud cheers from our forces. I dare say the
enemy was puzzled enough to know what we were
cheering about, for the fog was as bad as cannon-
smoke. And soon after the advance of the British
forces were seen coming to meet us with fascines of
sugar-cane and scaling ladders. On they came, nearer
and nearer, as, in years before, their ancestors had
advanced upon the redoubts at Bunker-Hill. We
were prepared for them, and just as they were
nearing the ditch, the signal for firing was given.
From our embrasures, and from the top of the
cotton bags there issued a sheet of fire, which, as
the loaded rifles were passed from behind in exchange for the discharged ones, became continual.
I was at the right flank among the cavalry, and it
seemed as if a row of furnaces were giving out
their red heat. The enemy were stricken as with
one single concentrated blow. Every other man
in the ranks had fallen; and throwing down fascines and ladders the brave fellows who were left
hastened back to their comrades. There was a
brief pause. The stragglers were rallied, and fresh
roops supported them. Again they rushed at the

sheets of liquid fire which our forces continued to pour forth. You would have thought our men had breakfasted on lead and made coffee out of powder for years, so cool were they with cannon and rifle. On came the British. But it was no battle. Although the balls of their muskets whistled merrily over our heads and plumped into the clay and the wedged cotton at our feet, the slaughter was all on one side. Yet they came on with brave impetuosity. Some of them pulled off their shoes to afford better foothold and jumped into the ditch to clamber over our position ; but as they came up by hundreds, the rifles of the Tennesseeans picked them off as if they had been black-birds. They charged—officers and privates indiscriminately—to the very muzzles of our guns, only to fall back lifeless or desperately wounded into the damp and muddy ditch—which was literally filled with bodies. Their onset was so impetuous at our flank by the river-side that some of them clambered on the wall (to so call it) and penetrated into camp, where the survivors were surrounded and taken prisoners. I shall never forget the look of one noble officer—a colonel of the line—as he jumped on a cotton bag, exclaiming, "courage, boys, we have them"—only to fall back the next minute with a rifle-ball in his brain. Three times the enemy came up manfully to the attack ; and, I believe, if Generals Pakenham and Keane had kept whole bodies, the advance would have continued until the army was half destroyed. As it was, seven hundred of them were killed, and some fourteen hundred wounded. Our own casualties did not reach seventy-five altogether.

We all thought they would renew the attack; for at nightfall they kept their camp-fires briskly burning, and were engaged in making batteries. But these latter were but designed to cover their retreat, which was commenced that night unmolested by us. Some generals might have quitted entrenchments to paralyse them yet more, thus disabled and in retreat. But Jackson was content to let well alone. A battle won with a clean list of killed or wounded is better than a distinguished victory where losses are met with. So ended the Battle of New Orleans.

M. The last engagement of any conseqnence upon American soil. May it continue the last.

Puff—puff—came along the little locomotive and its long car behind; and re-taking seats we forgot our military sighings in the discussion for the benefit of a fat friend on an adjoining seat, of the momentous question whether it was orthodox to eat rum-omelette with " pompano"-fish.

XVIII.

The Press of New Orleans.

LITERATURE in New Orleans *has been* a great deal like a moss rose in a plantation of Canada thistles.

But since the American portion of the citizens have reclaimed a thousand acres of swamp, and patronized granite for pavements, and catalogued some enterprising citizens, (the best of whom are the least talked about,) and since, too, the Saxons of the Second Municipality have rescued from the Gauls of the First Municipality a bank or so and a brace of railroads, (abused heretofore in these papers,) the said literature is a recognized and talked of thing in the Crescent City.

If we felt disposed to give some of the citizens (as the result of humble inquiries) some statistics of the authors and "authorlings," bards and "bardlings," and general writers who are covered up

with calculations in the " cotton and sugar line,"
and practical investigations into political economy,
as well as the results effected by certain daring
ones of those who have ventured to believe that a
man who could conceive a pleasant story, or throw
off a light-hearted sonnet, was not unfitted for
"'change," Crescent citizens might stare a little and
be vain to think that letters flourished so well
among swamps and English brokers. But we in-
tend no directory for home departments, nor guide-
book for strangers.

Not the least effective for the cause of letters in
New Orleans are its newspapers.

Certain of these for many years back have possessed very distinctive and celebrated characteristics.

There is no reason why every gazette, like every
novel, (we here exclude Mr. James,) should not
possess its peculiar features. But I submit it as a
" fixed fact," that there is scarcely one out of every
score which marks itself differently from its contemporaries. Every nineteen are apparently " got
up" out of the same inkstand, and " worked off"
on the same press. The type may be different, the
advertisers may vary, and the politics may be
" buff," or "blue ;" but as regards rhetoric, vigor
of thought, and originality of conception, they are
in the same dead level.

There is not division of labor enough among
their conductors, and the *one* newspaper in the

score possessing distinctive features is generally
presided over by a rare exception of versatility.
Newspaper talent nowadays is too much scattered.
If the sheriff could shut up a hundred or two establishments, and if the best of the editors thus
dis-executionized could be sifted out, and their
talent properly combined and distributed, we
might have that which we have not now, a paper
in the United States at half the cost, and twice the
excellence of the London Times; and editorials,
instead of being idiosyncrasies, would be essays
upon the history of the day worthy of posterity.

America has given the world a printing press
which is emblazoned in the History of Art. Who
will next bid arise in her borders a Joint Stock
Company for the publication of a newspaper, paying liberally for good gazette rhetoric, and so enrich the stockholders while benefitting society with
a *good* newspaper?

It was the New Orleans Picayune newspaper
which first gave a tone to the Crescent City press.
In its infancy, it was an audacious little sheet; and
when it came among its heavy-headed, half French,
half naturalized compeers, created an impression
something like that of a lively pin-wheel of a fire-
work evening in the midst of some complicated as-
sortment of powder and sulphur, bolstered up by a
dozen hickory poles. It dared to joke with sugar,
and to treat cotton as a light affair. It sneezed at
tobacco, and waxed merry in the midst of tallow

and ship chandlery. It wrote sonnets upon grave officials, who were accustomed to universal homage. Scarcely large enough to wrap around a loaf of bread, it was as full of witticisms as one of Thackeray's dreams after a light supper. It picked the locks of municipal portfolios, and sported with criminal justice. It taught the recorder that he was a born wit, and that the true way to enjoy his situation was to extract fun out of every prisoner arraigned. It woke up the captains of the police guard, and taught them to be funny. It ran with race-horses, and picked up all the good sayings on the turf. It lounged about the Levee, and hunted out rats and loafers with puns. In its office was a kaleidoscope, wherein every-day thoughts and every-day occurrences took new hues and curious combinations. If you saw a good thing floating over the country, making merry the farmers by their harvest-door loungings or apple-browning firesides, or travellers who forgot to yawn on steamboats and on railways, and serving, with larger newspapers, as the raisin in cider bottles, to work into effervesence—you were sure to notice, at the conclusion, as inevitable as the word "Bacon" to a vigorous excerpt—"*N. O. Pic.*"

" Who were the editors?" asked the outsiders :
" ' Phazma' and ' Straws,' " replied the Crescenter.

He was sure every one must know them. Not know the Brothers Field? Jim Fields, who had kept audiences in boxes and pit on the roar by the hour, and who had turned editor? Or Mat Fields, his sedater brother, whose heart was like a well, and deep enough for any honest human bucket to descend and take a draught of pure, reviving, sparkling friendship. Not know these? why, where was the use of living?

"'Phazma' and 'Straws' are poets, sir," he would continue; "none of your sleepy ones, who weave their doleful cantos as a sawney Scotchman weaves his rag carpet, with motley hues, but heavy texture; none of your namby-pamby ones, who talk to sensible merchants of honeysuckles and frisking lambs; none of your blubbering ones, who weep over human nature in lines like a yard-stick; but poets who eat rhyme, talk rhyme, and think rhyme, and who only have to shake their heads a little and out pop the sparkling thoughts, musically tripping over the paper on all the oddest topics, which an opium eater would scarcely dream of. Belligerent poets, too, sir! It was a perpetual suit they waged in the Court of the Muses. 'Phazma *versus* Straws.' Now one plaintiff in error—now the other. Now one repellant—now the same one respondent. Law and fact, sir, every inch of it. Do you think I could eat my muffins of the foggy groggy December mornings, when the air about the Levee was as thick as the mouth of a coal-pit, or enjoy my 'Pompano'-fish and rum omelette at the Lake End without dipping into a sonnet or the

stanzas, or the what-not-metre of the belligerents?
No, sir."

"Phazma and Straws!" With "Kendall" to
unbottle the tact, and "Lumsden" to distribute it
with untiring industry, the four raised a paper from
experiments to magnificent success. Everybody
was reading it; so everybody must advertise in it.
Besides it made its appearance of a Sunday morning, when your day of rest gives best inclination
to read, and omitted the Monday issue to give the
Sabbath to the writers and the pressman, in a sensible way. It couldn't avoid success no more than
clever girlhood can avoid a husband.

Kendall, too, had his days and nights of adventure on the prairies, and in the Texan fights, and
in the far-off odious Mexican captivity. His adventure spiced the paper, and took the edge off
all ill humor when the cargo missed its ports, or
cotton fell from the notch the foreigners last hung
it at.

"Straws" and "Phazma" left it. The pens of
heavy artillery now hunted for its columns. Its
champagne became rich port. Recorders' Courts
and Levee Scenes were handed over to ambitious
reporters to whom the connection was to be a capital, like "student of Sir Astley Cooper," or law-
clerk with the then Attorney General Butler to
your sawbones and brief-perusers. The paper
waxed dignified in its growing age, and punned
but now and then.

"Phazma" shortly after died, with the love of the beautiful and the appreciation of the grotesque as strong as ever; nothing dimmed by mortal conflict with that stern-faced ravager which steals away the breath while yet it plants fallacious roses on the cheeks.

"Straws" "drummed" subscribers with his telling and artistic "Reveille" in St. Louis. Kendall returned from captivity to be famous and write books. Lumsden held the reins of business, and had his turn of published adventure on the Rio Grande, and in the mountain-fastnesses of Mexico, amid all the stirring scenes which gave a name to one who died to make Death yet more illustrious as the conqueror of victors. Other partners less known, but as sturdy workers, shared in the prosperity. "Porter," the facetious, died at his post, and the laughers in his time of merry health have ever since worn in their memories the weeds of cordial regret.

Precocious and sprightly as it was in its youth, the "Pic" is dignified and eloquent in its growing age. "May its shadow never be less."

I was in the cabin of the tow-boat, which was "table-spooning" our gallant ship up the Mississippi, as narrated in a previous sketch, when I first saw a number of the "New Orleans Delta," got up and printed since my leaving Manhattan, by a graduate of the Picayune office. The type was good; the reading smelt freshly; the jokes were creditable ; and the items of the day served up with piquant sauce. The name, too, was characteristic and local, like "Picayune," and like the Delta of the Mississippi, many-mouthed ; nor the less valuable for being classical.

"This will do," cried a passenger, nodding approval self-complacently over my shoulder.

I was of his opinion, and he, poor fellow, had not seen a paper in a three week's passage ; so I forgave him the impoliteness.

The "Delta" commenced its career like a runaway schoolboy. It asked favors of nobody, but made itself known by a series of bold adventurings in the meadows of items, and the shrubbery of gossip. It despoiled the orchards of " exclusivism" of their holiday fruit. It brought the eye-glass of wondering merchants from vest pockets to look at the impudent sheet. Politicians laid in wait the newsboys (who liked the name, and rang all possible changes on the second syllable) to see what new joke was perpetrated on themselves or adversaries.

The "Picayune" had always joked at classes, or run the saw on " genera." The "Delta" singled out individual characteristics and spitted "species." The one, if it threw snuff in the eyes, courteously begged pardon for the offence ; the other took one eye at a time for the operation, and laughed at the mishap. Not that you could ever indict it for malicious prosecution. It took care to have a sem-

9

blance of probable cause, and be too good-humored
for malice.

Not a town topic existed but the "Delta" treated it. It talked with readers as readers talked
among themselves, boldly and unreservedly. It
set expediency at defiance; it listened to no coun-
sellings. Like a spoiled child it had its own way
with everybody.

Nothing is too "radical" for its swallow. Its
columns are open to "the people." Kid gloves it
professes to cleanse by a new process (caustic pot-
ash) which is sure to eat into the material at the
same time. It has its editors, but not half a dozen
subscribers could say who they were. It rallies
around it a corps of writers, who, by the prodigal
display they make of it, have not learned Saxon
for nothing. There is poetry enough in its columns year by year to make a dozen Appendixes
to Griswold's Poetry of America; dramatic criticisms which have the merit of plain talk, and
which court no favors; and dry jokes that are of
great importance to the country subscribers who
attend barbecues, and are expected to lead the
"toasts." The pens in its employ possess facility
of rhetoric not the least remarkable for their un-
weariedness of excellence. (This facility some day
will be fatal, if for one week the "judgment" leaves
its stand behind the counter.)

It is eminently a universal paper. For the lawyer
the "Delta" has its court scenes and counsel jokes.

For the doctor its ounces of good-natured sarcasm
and solid advice. For blundering officials its
cushion of thistles. For popular excitement its
quota of enthusiasm. For the clergy a dose of
brimstone or iced punch, at choice. For the planter's fireside its epitome of city items ready spiced
for the family reading. For the merchant its saws
on the tricks of trade.

The "Picayune" and "Delta" are the exponents
abroad of the New Orleans press, and therefore I
have selected them from the host of well conducted
journals for which the city is celebrated. Some
have chosen to think them rivals. I humbly conceive this can never be; although it is probable
had there never been a "Pic." there never would
have been a "Delta." The one is rigid in its
propriety without sacrificing its piquancy; the
other will have its joke, though the whole establishment go to the —— sheriff the next day in a
suit for libel. The one has for rule the safe one of
"policy;" to the other its dictionary knows no
such word. As I said before, the "Delta," like a
spoiled child, has always had its own way, and
ever will have, so long as strong Levees render sub-
marine apparatus useless commodities in the Crescent City.

The New Orleans "Commercial Bulletin" sus-
tains to the mercantile community of its locale the
same position occupid by the "Courier" and "Ad-
vertiser" at Boston; or the "Courier and En-

quirer" and "Journal of Commerce" at New
York; its editorials aim rather at the solidity of
dignified comment than at the piquancy of gossip;
its policy is eminently national and conservative;
and its advertising columns are grand bazaars of
trade wherein merchants "set forth" their wares by
the million-dollar-worth.

The "Courier" and the "Bee" (L'Abeille) are
papers chiefly in the Franco-American interest, and
for northerners in the Crescent City emulous of ac-
quiring the reading of French are capital exercises
—the "matter" of the French sides being rendered on the reverse of their sheets into Saxon. If
all the articles of these Gazettes possessed the brilliancy and spirit of their opera-critiques there
would be no "Daily" in New Orleans more in demand for "Exchange."

The "Delta" since its establishment has boiled
over twice; and the "Crescent" and "True Delta"
have emerged from the overflow. The former has
already grown like an Anak; and the parent
source may well be nerved to greater exertions,
lest in time to come, as regards both the last-named
Gazettes, its subscribers remind it of the old
rhyme :—

"To teach his grandson draughts, his leisure he'd employ,
 Until, at last, the old man was beaten by the boy."

XIX.

Leaving New Orleans River-ward.

WHITHER bound, *mon ami?*" said I, one morning, to an acquaintance whom I found airing a carpet-bag in the portico of the St. Charles Hotel.

"I'm taking my bag to have a little repairing done to the lock, for I think of taking 'a-run'-up to Louisville this afternoon."

"A run—to Louisville—why, it's a thousand miles—and only a carpet-bag!" stammered I.

"Pooh, pooh!" he rejoined, mumbling his after-breakfast cigar with great nonchalance, "that's nothing after you've lived in these parts a few years. Why, M—— went to Europe yesterday on two hours' notice, and will be back almost as quickly as you will reach Manhattan if you play sight-seer by the wayside. Splendid boat this afternoon, too—Peytona—a regular steam race-horse."

"I'm sorry I'd not known this before. I was going myself in a day or two, as soon as I found a boat."

"Found a boat! Come, now, that's good! Do you go looking after them with a telescope? Why, my boy, there's twenty at the Levee any day. I'll introduce you to one of our old stagers, one of the first merchants, who thinks it a capital joke when he hears the last bell of a steamboat ringing, to get quietly up from his counting-house desk, lock his drawers, and tell his clerks he's going to Vicksburg, just as coolly as he informs them of an absence to dinner. And that isn't all: he either steps on board just as the boat pushes off, or takes a small boat after her. Bound to go when he says so. Come up with your luggage; the clerk's a particular friend, and I'll promise you the best of state-rooms and fare."

"I'll do it," said I, grasping his hand.

And we met in the early evening on the "Peytona."

I had not been used to stepping on board just at shoving off, nor had I quite accustomed my comprehension to the calling a four or five day's sailing "a run," so I was down, with ample time to spare, and stood upon the boiler-deck, surveying the prospect, by the side of a nervous man, who declared he could feel the steam through his boots.

If ever there existed a commercial beehive, here was one: clerks, porters, draymen, hackmen, stevedores, deck-hands, passengers, and loafers, swarming in and out the cellular passages by the grain and cotton bags, hoghsheads, and corn sacks, far as the eye could reach. A dozen bells were ringing like mad, and the air was dark with the smoke from the firing-up of the dozen steamboats about, which lay side by side, head up to the piles of the Levee, like a column of marine soldiery. All about their stems and sterns, audaciously dashing under the very wheel-paddles, were scores of little boats filled with pedlary. The Jew was there with his hundred-bladed penknives, sponges, and metallic tablets; the Yankee with his curious knick-knacks brought from every auction mart in town; nondescripts with oranges, bananas, and conch-shells, which latter, now and then, were blown with sound resembling the bray of a mule when touched with colic, to which the steamboat bells tolled out their music exultingly.

"D'ye see that boat, the third from us?" asked my *compagnon du voyage*, who now had joined the throng about us.

"She with the heaviest smoke and loudest bell?"

"The same."

"She'll beat us on the start. How eager to push off!"

My friend gave me one of his peculiar laughs, and added, "If she backs out into the stream before day after to-morrow, I'll forfeit your good opinion. That puffing, and wheezing, and bell-tolling is all a sham—a trick to catch passengers. She's the only boat of her trade in, and will keep up the fuss until every other neighboring steamer has left; then her smoking, and wheezing, and bell-tolling will cease until to-morrow afternoon, when a second edition will be issued, and so on till some other of the line is up. It's a regular thing with some boats."

"And do the public stand it?"

"*Her* public have to; she's Hobson's choice to-day. Do you remember Tom ——, he who played the Kent bugle so effectually at Captain Ric's last concert? He was once on board of her when all this fuss was going on. By-and-by, both captain and pilot were ashore some distance off, and Tom mounted to the wheel-house, for he's a bit of an amateur pilot, as he is an amateur in music. Wink-ing to two or three of his friends on the Levee, off went the lines; the wheels were revolving back-ward at the time furiously, and off she spun into the river, upsetting a brace of fat darkies who were carrying supplies aboard, and sending a dozen conch-shells from a little wherry behind, to amuse the mermaids and catfish below. 'Stop her!' cried the captain, running to the water's edge and ges-ticulating furiously. The pilot fell to swearing, (as all pilots do in emergencies,) and the crowd about hurrahed. Tom headed her up river, and away she went for a few lengths, but he hadn't calculated the current; and the first thing he knew, he was against a seven hundred tonner, just in, full of Dutch emigrants, battering against her sober sides like a battering-ram at the walls of Jerusalem, and frightening the poor jaw-breaking linguists out of their senses.

"It took Tom some time to work out of that scrape. Old ——, who was then District Attorney, gave it as his opinion that the proceeding was 'flat piracy;' but he couldn't find a Grand Jury to do anything but laugh at him, and call it a good joke. But here we are off."

And the Peytona spun into the stream like a mettled courser at the drum-tap. She was evidently puffed with self-conceit of her own power and ability; for not a stair deigned to creak under the loads of baggage and fat humanity which had hurried up and down from deck to deck; not an inch of carpet in the splendid saloon had dimmed beneath the tread of passengers; her smoke belched upward with all the pomposity of furnace-kindling; and her wheels beat the turbid waters with solid pats which were intended to strike suitable terror into the mammoth catfish round about.

The "Peytona" was built like all other Western river steamboats, with an elliptical hull beaten out at the poles more than is geometrical in an ellipse, and upon the hull sat the machinery, duly imprisoned and overlaid by the mansion-like cabin, which was pillared up from bow to stern. A flight of steps from the water's edge gave passage to the boiler-deck and entrance to the two saloons beyond. Still another deck was over the inclosed cabin, whither the captain and pilot went into appropriate exile whenever the boat was on its winding way, and where children gamboled, (is vice so young on the Mississippi River, I think I hear some listener say,) while their papas smoked in active opposition to the puffing escape pipes at their side.

We swept by the city. A mile or so of shipping to eye, with here and there some caravanserai, like cotton-yards, and the houses had longer separation between them. Here was Lafayette, the asylum of anglicised Dutchmen—next we bent into Carrollton—and then commenced the monotonous scenery of the Mississippi River—flat land and winding river, trees and sedgy grass, with occasionally a bit of bluff, with elevation like the snow-hills your school-boy builds in the midst of a New Hampshire winter.

Night came on, and with it the tea-urn—after which I plunged into a state-room, arranged my wardrobe for the next four days, and settled down to sleep, thinking of "Longfellow" in the narrow berth, and his poetry, especially of the lines—

> Not enjoyment, and not sorrow,
> Is my destined end or way;
> But to live that each to-morrow
> *Finds me further than to-day.*

Further up the Mississippi, of course.

One day upon a Mississippi steamboat is generally a stereotype of all the other days of passage. There may sometimes occur a snagging, or a fire, with perhaps a collision, to vary the incidents of each sluggish hour; but since the river navigation is so well understood, and captains and pilots, by becoming owners of the crafts they guide, are more careful, a total want of catastrophe is the most expectable by even nervous ladies.

One day, then, is the sample of all—and how does it wear away?

The dull light of morning becomes brighter and roseate over the tree-tops about, as the steam-packet still puffs and paddles her way along.

As the sun emerges from the forests about, sleepy travellers emerge from their state-room doors on the outside guard passage-way, and in every variety of demi-toilette, swallow the fresh air. A heavy-eyelided negro will be scattering dust in the cabin with serious intentions of accomplishing the operation usually termed "sweeping." Another of the same description will be summoning courage for the exertion of shaking the large cabin-bell, whose sound is intended to diminish a passenger's quota of sleep. Other sleepy waiters will emerge from unknown parts of the boat, and attend to the complicated machinery of the table; which by their exertions (although five minutes before it had scarcely afforded room for the lounging legs of a

Hoosier,) soon becomes a long table ready for breakfast, dinner, or supper, at the appropriate hours for each meal. At the noise of the clicking plates, and rattling knives and forks, the hungry passengers from door-gaping state-rooms, and from side doors, and through the windows from the hurricane-deck, watch with stomachic interest the evolutions of the waiters. They anathematize the laziness of this one, or commend the briskness of that one. They count the plates, and endeavor to smell out the bill of fare as opens the pantry door. And with their eyes they measure the bread which the cabin-boy carefully puts out by every plate, delicately plunging a fork into an immense bread-tray full of bread-chunks, and then executing a quit-claim by a dexterous shove of his dexter fore-finger. By degrees there accumulate before the watching eyes hot corn-bread and rolls, steaks and chops, while pitchers of milk and basins of sugar are deployed in the centre of the table. A fat waiter enters with a coffee urn, which is bubbling musically. A retinue of leaner waiters, similarly armed, with now and then an urn of tea, follow him. Diffident passengers edge slowly up. The " old travellers " march toward the head of the table with confident air, and selecting a particular chair, stand behind it and eye it as if determined to risk life itself before surrender-ing up a seat or missing the first dive at a beef-steak and plate of rolls. Other gentlemen have walked towards that steamboat sanctum sanctorum ycleped ladies' saloon, and self-complacently watch the opening doors, for well they know THEY have a seat reserved. The hungry diffidents and "old uns" below are eyeing with envious sullenness these aforesaid reserved seats and their reserved future occupants. Presently the captain descends from his place of exile on the hurricane-deck, takes off his hat, and polishes his red forehead with a still redder handkerchief, and marches dignifiedly to the top of the table, followed by admiring eyes at the foot. The admiring eyes soon reassume an hungry aspect. The bell rings, and down drop the passengers and proceed to attack the edibles. The ladies' table is a complete battle-field of affectation struggling with the appetite which a river-breeze induces. Steamboat coffee is criticised—biscuits are nibbled—and perhaps, in a certain quarter, a plate of hot rolls furnishes text for an anti-dyspeptic lecture from an old lady, to whom dry toast proves a great consolation.

Breakfast over, the ladies retire to their toilette, or their lace and worsted work, or perchance a book; others of them enliven the cabin with music from the grand piano which every first-class boat provides for company. The gentlemen seek the boiler deck, where they sit in gaping arm-chairs, and talk, or read in their books with colored covers the various wonders of modern romance; or hang their legs over the rail and smoke in musing silence as they gaze at the scenery about.

Politics is the prevailing theme; although now and then a reckoning of distances affords an exciting topic of conversation for the moment. The waiters within have taken to pieces the complicated table machinery, only to put the pieces together again in a few hours. At one of the bits of table there is card-playing. Some gamblers are near by watching an opportunity to join the party. But they are compelled to be cautious and diplomatic; for gambling on the western waters, like watch-stuffing in goodly Manhattan, has come to be understood; and there is little card-fleecing nowaday on the Mississippi first-class packets. At another table a bilious-looking youth is endeavoring to write; but gives up in despair upon hearing a passer-by remark, *sotto voce* to a friend, " how proficient that young man is in short-hand hieroglyphics." At another table some infatuated youths have commenced a game of chess; but before five moves a castle urged by the shaking boat as she labors over a sand bar, and which was still hemmed in by unmoved pieces, gives check by a strange freak, and bishops and knights prance about merrily.

On drives the boat; perhaps stopping " on a swamp-bound coast" to land a passenger or take one up; in either case shoving a narrow plank ashore and sending him to walk it as if both himself and plank were troubled with an ague fit no patent medicine could palliate. Or the boat stops at some town or city builded almost among a primeval forest; and the passengers step ashore to stretch their legs and walk a bit through the town or buy refreshments.

Or the boat hungers for wood, and at a given signal there pushes out from the river bank a flat boat loaded with a dozen cords. A line is thrown and the flat boat made fast to the steamer's side, where the wood soon changes position without any loss of time save in speed diminished by towing along additional floating matter. The wood unloaded, the lines are cut, and the flat boat floats back to its station.

Lunch is an agreeable interlude. So is dinner; and the siesta in the hot cabin. Or the afternoon lounge by the favored few in the ladies' cabin, where there is of course the usual variety of nonsense, flirtation, and music. Or the watching the daylight fade as promenading the hurricane deck. Then rings the tea-bell. There is more eating and drinking. The cards thereafter shuffle brisker at the table by the bar; and the laughter and fun in the ladies' cabin sounds better from beneath the brilliant lights. Then comes sleep; and closes a day the like of which you will see to-morrow, and as long thereafter as circumstances and low water keep you under headway.

Low water!

I gathered some experience as to the meaning of that phrase after getting into the Ohio. Our skilful pilot had brought us past a half dozen of boats smaller than our own who were aground; many of them, however, very distinguished in a general way. There was the "General Scott," puffing and blowing on a sand-bar with all its fires foremost. There was the General Worth, and the General Taylor, and the General Washington, all striking their flags at two or three feet of water, covered with the ignominy of our passing shrugs and laugh. But the turn of the "Peytona" came next; and with a bump which threw the head-steward into the door of a state-room he was entering among a parcel of trunks; and brought powerful groans from all the freight of nervousness on board; and upset the calculations of a trio of amateur sharpers who were being pigeoned by their would-be-victim, the boat "brought up" on a sand-bar.

"More steam" was the word passed to the engineer; while the heaviest of the passengers held a mass meeting in the stern to lighten the weight of the boat on the bar, and thus enable the boat to back out and feel a better channel. Swifter and swifter revolved the paddles; fire flashed from the furnace-eyes of the "Peytona;" she was spurred to the utmost of her powers; but "the nature of the course proved too much." A flat boat was near at hand and the usual business of lightening cargo by throwing us overboard—don't stare—into the said flat boat was immediately resorted to. The latter was soon filled with her male cargo, leaving the ladies and babies on board; thus forming a sort of nautical Methodist assemblage. The proceeding answered, and the good river Ohio, no doubt, pleased with this offering of man's pride to the power of her channel, lowered the sands beneath us and over the bar we went.

Of all places in the world for the study of humanity in all its variety of light and shade, in all its grotesqueness, picturesqueness, and kaleidoscope changes of charater, give me the Mississippi steamboat. Industrious patronage of Manhattan omnibuses, particularly the line which boast the guardianship of town-renowned "Kipp & Brown," or of the Harlem Railroad cars below "Twenty-Seventh street," may do something for the "proper study of mankind." I am not sure but that diligent pursuit of novelty in the direction of our city suburb, "Hoboken," of summer afternoons, may be of benefit in the same line. But travel on the Mississippi River and you will give the palm to its steamboats. Here meet all the grades of life; a thousand chapters of human history bind themselves ever in the cabins, capable on slight acquaintance of an interesting reading; human passion in every variety turns its sides for inspection. A week of contact rubs off the outer coatings of selfishness; picks the locks of mind; unfolds a score of conventional heart-coverings; lays bare a thousand tricks of life; and fills your book of mental observation with curious and valuable notes and addenda for reference.

Let no Manhattaner hankering after foreign travel neglect to "voyage it" on the western waters before breathing European air.

APPENDIX.

---◄●●►---

THE individual here alluded to—Mr. John McDonough—has deceased while these pages are passing through the press; and as the newspapers have made his name, peculiarities, and circumstances of life and death somewhat notorious, I beg leave to add a few of my personal reminiscences concerning him.

During my visit to New Orleans my attention became early attracted to a tall gaunt figure, which, clad in a suit of blue cloth—the coat having brass buttons—surmounted by a rather faded hat; the neck covered by a white neck-'kerchief, not of the most spotless hue; which tightly grasping in its hand the handle of a green umbrella sculled through the streets at a rapid rate. This was Mr. McDonough, the deceased Millionaire. In his soulless face, and chilliness of demeanor, he realized, more than any other I ever saw, the idea of Douglass Jerrold's, "The Man of Money." In many respects he was exceedingly like the character just alluded to. And even before reading that novel I had fashioned Mr. McDonough to my own fancy, as a man whose heart was exhausted of human blood, and beating alone from the instinct of monied interest; whose strength of body and mind decayed with every dollar that he spent.

Upon inquiry of the *habitues* of the city into the history of this strange personage, I learned he was a native of Baltimore, which city he had quitted at the age of twenty-one to settle in the then far off province of Louisiana. That, reaching New Orleans, he had embarked in successful trade; and had ever since lived but for the one purpose—of amassing wealth. That he resided in the cheerless district of Algiers; denying himself the ordinary comforts of life; destitute of society; seeking no acquaintances; asking no favors; dead to the commoner feelings of humanity; and grasping and overbearing in all his intercourse with his fellow-man. Apparently without a relation in the world; friendless, for he had no heart wherein to nourish a generous impulse; without an enemy, indeed, because none could hate, where there was so much to pity. In this manner he had lived for over half a century; and was as much a part of Franco-American Louisiana as the bogs of its soil or the fogs of its swamps, and, indeed, not unlike them in the cheerless influence of his presence. Of himself he would at times talk quite freely, but it was always of what he was going to do in the future, not of what he had effected or was doing. His personal expenses being somewhat less than that of an ordinary coal-heaver, he was enabled to accumulate, year by year, landed property, which is now supposed to be in value some millions of dollars. If he was seen to ride in an omnibus, the circumstance was chronicled by the gossipers as an event. He was once known to purchase an orange; but the huxter-woman from whom he bought it was ever afterwards remarkable for her ill-luck. Although the ferriage from his place to New Orleans cost but a trifle, whenever he visited the city, he was accustomed to be rowed across the rapid current of the river in a frail skiff. Returning home he immediately divested himself of his characteristic habiliments, and put his appearance on a par with that of his commonest negro slave.

He was a man of considerable education; of great business sagacity; shrewd and quick in calculation; and a logical capi-

talist. So that his ends were attained, he had no scruple for the
means; and in the purchase of a large quantity of city bonds,
and the ratification of their sale, through the influence of a
judge—who afterwards fled from the city in dire disgrace—
there lives a mystery, which none can unravel, but which, if
seen through, would probably result in an unfavorable aspect
for the deceased *millionaire*. He died in the latter end of October, 1850, from a sudden attack of bilious colic. The new-
est stranger in town had scarcely ceased to wonder at the
outre appearance of the miser who he had just seen, when he
learned the fact of his death. It was extensively known
through the city that Mr. McDonough entertained very peculiar ideas concerning the bequest of his vast estate. With an
affectation of piety, to the sincerity of which every outward
action of his life gave the most palpable lie, he had announced
that he was but accumulating property for the Lord. For
many days speculation was rife as to the contents of his will.
What disinterestedness was to be expected from it may be
easily guessed at, when one remembers, that at one era in his
life-time he demanded praise from the philanthropic world for
freeing a ship-load of negroes, and sending them to Africa,
whom, in truth, he had compelled to the purchase of themselves at his own premium valuation. On opening the will, it
was discovered that several millions in value of his landed property, were directed to be held in trust for the purpose of
founding an eleemosynary institution in his native State; while
he had left but the most miserable pittance to the blood-rela-
tions, to whom in his life-time, he had "turned the cold shoulder." These, however, were on the watch for a descent upon
his peculiarities of testamentary disposition, for the purpose of
recognizing, through the medium of law, their claims to a portion of their miserly kinsman's earnings. Without being
allowed more than a cursory glance at the detail of his will, I
should think that those portions of it, which lock up his vast
estate—perhaps with a cheating of the State in the matter of

taxation, while it is held for charitable purposes—are contrary
to the civil law jurisprudence of Louisiana, where all bequests
in the nature of *fidei commissa* are prohibited. The lawyers and
notaries of his adopted city will now have an opportunity of
fully sharing disbursements from an estate which was so jeal-
ously guarded from legal encroachments. The most superfi-
cial observer would say, that unless the nut was certain to be
cracked, so many legal hammers would not be put in requisi-
tion, when the prospect of extrinsic emolument was so slight
—the heirs being as poor in creature comforts as was their
ancestor, although not with the same choice.

Some may plead to my declarations the classical statute of
limitations which recites " *de mortuis dicere nil nisi bonum*,
but to the universality of this maxim I beg leave to respect-
fully demur.

If the life of a man, in praise of whom the tongue must be
silent, affords any instructive lesson, it is the duty of all to pro-
fit by its narration.   And the life of Mr. McDonough certainly
teaches his contemporaries and posterity that Christian charity
should oftenest adorn every day life and character. That to
neglect the commoner instincts of humanity unto an old age,
in order to build up a selfish monument of posthumous fame,
is no way to satisfy the purposes of probationary existence; or
to balance accounts with the Almighty power, whose blessings
were so bounteously poured out upon their unworthy re-
cipient.

INDEX

DATE DUE